Reconstructing Democracy, Recontextualizing Dewey

Reconstructing Democracy, Recontextualizing Dewey

Pragmatism and Interactive Constructivism in the Twenty-first Century

EDITED BY
Jim Garrison

STATE UNIVERSITY OF NEW YORK PRESS

Published by
State University of New York Press, Albany

For information, contact State University of New York Press, Albany, NY
www.sunypress.edu

Production by Diane Ganeles
Marketing by Anne M. Valentine

Library of Congress Cataloging-in-Publication Data

Reconstructing democracy, recontextualizing dewey : pragmatism and
interactive constructivism in the twenty-first century / [edited by]
Jim Garrison
    p. cm.
Includes bibliographical references and index.
ISBN 978–0–7914–7545–4 (hardcover : alk. paper)
ISBN 978–0–7914–7546–1 (paperback : alk. paper)
    1. Pragmatism. 2. Dewey, John, 1859–1952. 3. Constructivism
(Philosophy) 4. Democracy. I. Garrison, Jim, 1951–

B832.R38 2008
144′.3—dc22

                                                            2007044955

10 9 8 7 6 5 4 3 2 1

We dedicate this book to our dear friend and colleague, the late Hans Seigfried, whose enthusiasm we remember with gratitude and a great sense of loss.

Contents

Contents

Acknowledgments

Part of chapter 8 appeared earlier in *Dewey's Logical Theory: New Studies and Interpretations*, 2002, edited by F. Thomas Burke, D. Micah Hester, and Robert B. Talisse. Nashville: Vanderbilt University Press, and is reprinted with the permission of the publisher, Vanderbilt University Press.

Reconstructing Democracy and Recontextualizing Deweyan Pragmatism

Jim Garrison

Dewey, the neo-Darwinian, thought we lived in an ever-evolving world that required the continuous reconstruction of ideas and ideals to survive and thrive. The idea of democracy (along with the associated ideals of freedom, equality, and social justice, as well as the institutions—civil, religious, economic and such—for realizing them) is no exception. Dewey was a philosopher of reconstruction. Those who claim to understand Dewey yet do not reconstruct him for their time, place, and purpose fail to appreciate what was perhaps his most profound message. The chapters in this book recover and reconstruct Dewey for today's postmodern, post-9/11, fragmented, and globalized world.

According to Dewey, "The most pervasive fallacy of philosophic thinking goes back to neglect of context" (LW 6: 5).[1] He distinguishes two kinds of context: "background" and "selective interests." We will return to selective interests later. Background comes in two kinds, temporal and spatial.

1

"Temporal background" refers to entrenched traditions and culture customs along with each individual's habits of conduct
acquired through cultural participation. There is also a temporal
background of intellectual traditions that "differentiate it from
blind custom" (12). For Dewey, intelligence, especially reflective
and creative intelligence, which both critiques actual conditions
and imagines and constructs alternative conditions, is the key to
freedom. We liberate and control ourselves by comprehending
and controlling the world that conditions our conduct.

Each chapter in this book champions cooperative social
inquiry as being critical to the preservation and growth of
democracy. Two chapters, those by Larry A. Hickman and Hans
Seigfried, are devoted largely to democratic social inquiry.
"Spatial background" covers "all the contemporary setting
within which a course of thinking emerges" (13). The chapters
that appear in this book recontextualize Dewey in this way,
although they also are very aware of the temporal background
of their reconstructions. The intellectual tradition used to provide reconstructive reflection on Dewey's original democratic
constructions is his own pragmatic theory coupled on two occa-
sions with the original insights of Köln (Cologne) Interactive
Constructivism. Each contributor relies on some version of
Dewey's theory of inquiry, although there is disagreement about
its adequacy, which leads some to suggest reconstruction (see
Kersten Reich, Stefan Neubert, and Charlene Haddock
Seigfried) while others (see Larry A. Hickman and Hans
Seigfried) seek to illustrate its surprising breadth and depth.
Hickman, Neubert, and Reich are especially interested in draw-
ing educational consequences from Dewey's theory of inquiry,
whether reconstructed or not.

Let us pause and ask about our times, our present context.
What is the state of democracy today? Modern liberal democracies such as those established by the American and French revolutions assume an isolated, atomistic individual born with innate
free will, innate rationality, and innate natural rights. For
Dewey, freedom, rights, rationality, and individuality are contingent social constrictions dependent on intelligent inquiry,
and not innate endowments. For him, "Freedom or individuality, in short, is not an original possession or gift. It is something

to be achieved, to be wrought out" (LW 2: 61). Köln Interactive Constructivism, represented here in the chapters by Reich and Neubert, obviates these contingencies, as my chapter does, directly confronting the assumptions of liberalism regarding the constitution of personal identity. Although Dewey did not think human rights and the like were innate, he did think they were tremendous cultural achievements, part of our contemporary context, that should not only to be preserved but expanded. Freedom, rights, and intelligence are cultural and individual achievements for Dewey, not natural endowments. One is fortunate if they happen to be born in a nation where such accomplishments are part of the cultural background, while others must struggle for them. Dewey had a "socialist" view of liberalism that Judith Green calls particular attention to in her chapter, while Neubert and Garrison mention it in passing. It is a natural consequence of Dewey's social constructivist theory of mind and self that is discussed to some degree in all of the chapters in this book.

Today's neoliberals do not question any of the fundamental assumptions of liberalism, though they do tend to insist that all rationality is calculative and utilitarian instead of reflective, imaginative, and deliberative. Classic liberal economic theory was laissez-faire. Neoliberals recognize the role of Keynesian economics and the state in regulating the market, but following Milton Friedman and his mentor, Friedrich August von Hayek, they reject all other forms of socialism (e.g., social security, welfare, public schools, public health, etc.). The effect of neoliberalism is to limit the public commons to the marketplace and voting to market purchase. As Dewey said over seventy years ago, "Anthropologically speaking, we are living in a money culture. Its cult and rites dominate" (LW 5: 46). Public policy deliberation increasingly reduces to market calculation, which requires that everything have a quantitative price. Dewey's theory of social deliberation and inquiry counters this kind of reductionism. He did not anticipate the specifics of neoliberalism, but even in his day, he was aware that "our institutions, democratic in form, tended to favor in substance a privileged plutocracy," and he did not hesitate to place his hopes in "a socialized economy" (LW 11: 60, 63). On this and many other matters, Dewey provides a mirror upon which to reflect upon our own times, as well as some of the tools and insights needed to ameliorate the situation.

Today, there is an influential neoconservative movement perhaps most readily recognizable in the writings of Allen Bloom and his student, Francis Fukuyama. Bloom's mentor was Leo Strauss, who was influenced in turn by his teacher in Germany, Carl Schmitt (who was one of the architects of the Third Reich and author of the proposition granting the chancellor unlimited powers). Strauss himself believed in democracy, but only for those who were most fitted for it. According to the former student of Strauss, and later biographer, Anne Norton (2004), his work has spread through a tight network of highly influential students and disciples that currently number into the hundreds, all positioned at important spots in government, universities, corporations, and even military academies. She identifies such think tanks as the Olin, Scaife, Earhart, Lynde, and Harry Bradley foundations as bolstering and financing the movement with billions of dollars.

The neoconservatives, influenced by Plato's idea of philosopher kings, believe only a small elite has the wisdom to rule, because only they can bear the burden of the truth. The vulgar, however, have become so powerful in even our limited modern democracies that it is only possible to control them by indirection, using "the noble lie" conveyed by various media to shape the will of the people to the higher purposes of their leaders. Dewey wrote:

> Every autocratic and authoritarian scheme of social action rests on a belief that the needed intelligence is confined to a superior few who because of inherent natural gifts are endowed with the ability and the right to control the conduct of others; laying down principles and rules and directing the ways in which they are carried out. (LW 11: 219)

Dewey fought such elitist attitudes that emphasized democracy *for* the people but not *by* the people. He addressed such attitudes in his famous *The Public and Its Problems* (LW 2), which is the focus of James Campbell's lead chapter in this book. Dewey's hope was for a participatory democracy of the masses, which we will find articulated in every chapter that follows, although none mention the frightening specter of neoconservativism. For Dewey, the key to democracy is more liberating, creative, and critical learning, not miseducation for the multitude.

In many ways, neoconservatives recoil from the very idea of liberal modernity, and especially later modernity's notions of socialism and mass democracy, which they fear leads to relativism. Deweyan pragmatism, with its constructivist, conceptualist theory of universals (concepts, categories, rules, laws), falls far short of the kind of absolutism and fixity they demand. Nothing less than a Platonic ideal of the philosopher king who has seen the eternal Forms will satisfy them. (Larry A. Hickman's and Hans Seigfried's chapters expound upon Dewey's evolutionary theory of "scientific" concepts and its implications for moral concepts.) If anything is worse than modernism for neoconservatives, however, it is the rampant nominalism of postmodernism that denies the very possibility of unifying metanarratives while emphasizing endless diversity, difference, and fragmentation. Sometimes it also seems to flirt with nihilism. Deweyan pragmatism seeks dynamic and evolving unity in diversity, but it rejects the postmodern tendency to nominalism, fragmentation, and nihilism. Nonetheless, in their chapters, the two foremost representatives of Köln constructivism, Reich and Neubert, astutely show how postmodernism, properly employed, can help identify shortcomings in Dewey's philosophy of otherness and difference as well as his failure to fully theorize power, especially oppressive power.

Dewey also was prescient about the role of religion, spirituality, and morality in modern society. He signed "A Humanist Manifesto" in the spring of 1933, along with thirty-four professors, clergyman, and writers. Part of the humanist movement in religion, it affirmed evolutionary naturalism while rejecting supernaturalism, deism, theism, and personal immortality. The manifesto emphasized the function of religion in addressing human needs, the release of human creativity, the pursuit of social justice (the kingdom of heaven on earth), and "a socialized and co-operative economic order" (cited in Rockefeller 1991, 450). It simultaneously rejected religious fundamentalism and materialistic, atheistic, and secular humanism, such as one finds in classical Marxism, Freud, or the reductionism of logical empiricism. The chapters by Campbell, Green (with an emphasis on Dewey's metaphysics), and Hickman grapple directly with the contemporary legacy of Dewey's position, which was, perhaps, much more popular in his day than in ours. A creative tension among these chapters helps readers decide what they think about such matters for themselves.

One problem with fundamentalism (which only began around 1910), for Dewey, was that it had lost the numinous and allegorical sense of religion by thinking finite beings could grasp the literal truth of the infinite divine mystery. Another was that it often had ceased to pursue the kingdom of heaven on earth through works, while emphasizing dogmatic faith rewarded only in the afterlife. Dewey thought that, some aspects of religiosity were subject to intelligent inquiry, but, as Hickman notes, he was willing to acknowledge the religious experience, like aesthetic experience to which it is closely allied, as an immediate, noncognitive, consummatory experience in itself. Such immediately profound experience may be the source of material for inquiry but was not in itself an object of knowledge. Like all religious humanists, Dewey's spirituality sought intimate relation with existence wherein our creative acts matter in the course of creating cosmos from chaos.

Ours is a globalized world, an important part of the "spatial context" wherein the present chapters appear. Globalism refers to a constellation of economic, technological, social, cultural, and political changes involving increasing international interdependence, interaction, and integration. Some see it as a form of cultural and corporate imperialism and homogenation of diversity, or even both as the same thing.[2] On the other hand, globalism could lead to wider economic prosperity, international collaboration, and the creative use of differences. We believe the present volume represents a positive instance of global collaboration where pragmatism, a philosophy largely associated with the United States, interrelates with Köln Interactive Constructivism that relies on, critiques, and reconstructs Deweyan pragmatism to better fit its German and European context. The result is a work that expresses a critical-creative dialogue, across national and intellectual differences, that expresses well what a global democratic conversation might look like.

Thus far I have said nothing about the context of uniquely individual selective interests. Dewey insists: "There is selectivity (and rejection) found in every operation of thought. There is care, concern, implicated in every act of thought. There is some one who has affection for some things over others" (LW 6: 13). It is a mistake to assume that one's surroundings is one's environment. One's environment is what enters one's biological and social functioning. To what one does not attend either consciously or unconsciously, one cannot respond; it cannot influence one's conduct. All perspectives are partial and incomplete, something Haddock Seigfried makes much of in her chapter. Dewey further notes: "Interest, as the subjective, is after all equivalent to individuality or uniqueness" (14). Uniquely individual, emotionally influenced selective interests help set the immediate context of individual action, although we must remember not only individual needs and desires but also the temporal and spatial background of the culture(s) within which the individual participates. The chapters by Seigfried and Garrison both explore the all-too-often ignored embodied, emotional, and uniquely individual aspects of selective interests and their role in constituting personal identity within a pluralistic community.

The chapters in this book reflect the immediate interests of the nationalities of their authors, who are all European or North American. It is primarily a first world, North Atlantic perspective. An important part of responsible scholarship is to acknowledge, as we have, the context within which we write. Nonetheless, all of the chapters here, in one way or another, are interested in issues of difference, diversity, and inclusion. As pluralistic democrats, they all remain permanently open to creative encounters with others, although they acknowledge the difficulties. The issues raised and explored are readily recognizable to scholars globally.

Dewey identified and understood in his day many of the social, political, and economic forces still found hard at work in our time. He provides a temporal mirror for contemporary reflection, but we cannot effectively translate him into action until we understand and reconstruct him for our age. In this introduction, I have tried to describe some of the contemporary spatial and temporal contexts wherein the chapters gathered here will find their meaning in transaction with you, the reader, with your selective interests.

Campbell's "The Political Philosophy of Pragmatism" provides a good start for this collection. He begins by exploring six themes associated with Dewey's chief political work, *The Public and Its Problems* (LW 2). First, there is the appearance of this volume in a time of grave doubts in America about the possibilities of democracy, doubts that have now grown international and are expressed by others here. Anti-democrats, such as the so-called democratic realists in Dewey's day and the neoconservatives in ours, propose putting political matters into the hands of experts rather than the masses of people, whom they deemed incompetent to govern. Dewey rejected the claim that popular democracy had failed and proposed instead that what America really needed was more, not less, democracy. Campbell, following Dewey, rejects the claim that popular democracy had failed and proposes instead that what America really needs is more, not less, democracy. Second, Dewey asserted the primacy of the community over the individual in questions of social policy. For Dewey, publics, and eventually government, emerge when the indirect consequences of actions extend beyond those immediately engaged in producing them, so that those suffering the consequences have a legitimate interest in regulating them. The third theme involves a "pragmatic" understanding of the state as the community and its government that attempts to address the problems of shared living. For Dewey, the definition of the state is never a fixed and final form but always subject to revision. Fourth, Dewey emphasized the importance of maintaining the evolutionary flexibility of the state. Consequences emerge that were not there before, whereas other consequences cease and no longer require regulation. Because government, for Dewey, is a function and not a fixed essence, its scope, size, and shape must shift with the changing context. This implies that government in modern America suffers because of the conditions of historical liberalism present when it first emerged, and that it must evolve to respond to the present situation. Government should be an adaptive tool for solving the problems of our times. The fifth theme, consequent on the fourth, emphasizes the need for changes in the way that we think about and carry out our political practice. Every generation must learn to cautiously abandon their traditional stance and engage in deliberate intellectual and institutional reconstruction. They must learn to rethink democracy for their time and place. Finally, Dewey emphasized the fundamental necessity of faith in the possibility of cooperative inquiry to make democracy work. Campbell considers the contemporary situation in American society, where virtually all of Dewey's themes are neglected, and where political practice is driven by absolutism, oversimplification, partisanship, and chauvinism, and the vital communal life of democracy has withered. Campbell concludes that we need to return to procedures that are more communal if democracy is to flourish, but he finds reason to be skeptical about the possibility.

In her contribution, "Dr. Dewey's Deeply Democratic Metaphysical Therapeutic for the Post-9/11 American Democratic Disease: Toward Cultural Revitalization and Political Reinhabitation," Green expands on her theory of "deep democracy" developed in an earlier work. Here she examines the health of her nation and recommends a metaphysical therapeutic to restructure background assumptions within its current patterns of communication on the local, national, and international levels. She finds signs of disease in America's anxiety over the events of September 11, 2001, and the wars it has carried out in response. Green believes Americans still long for shared democratic hope, not only among themselves but also with citizens from around the world. Instead of pursuing the hope-fostering ways of democracy, however, widespread fears have led many Americans to place their trust in military might, totalitarian nationalism, torture, and demonizing all that seems different and strange. We are ailing, but we cannot seem to agree on what ails us or how to remedy it. Following Dewey, Green recommends pragmatist philosophical inquiry and reconstruction, which she believes will require employing a limited, context-specific democratic "metaphysic" to quite inquiry. She believes Dr. Dewey's curing system can alleviate a fourfold "democratic disease" now epidemic in America and the West: institutional subvertibility, ideological hollowness, individual nihilism, and cultural anomie. Green thinks Dewey's "metaphysic" provides a good physic for our poor health. Unlike traditional Western metaphysics of substance, of fixed form, and final essences, Green shows that Dewey advocated a process metaphysic that allows us to create and then recreate an inquiry-guiding and imagination-stirring "big picture" or "background map" of the world of humanly "experienced and experienceable" general traits or conditions that appear at any moment common to human existence and the wider natural world within which we live. Seeing philosophy as a "liaison officer" among different disciplines, it integrates and unifies by facilitating communicative action across diverse context-specific discourses. It allows us to reach out far beyond the academy and the problems of philosophers to address the wider problems of local, national, and global "publics" that we, as philosophers should serve.

In his contribution "Democracy and Education after Dewey—Pragmatist Implications for Constructivist Pedagogy," Reich calls on the resources of Köln Interactive Constructivism to supplement and reconstruct the two determining criteria of a desirable community, as originally formulated by Dewey in his 1916 *Democracy and Education* (MW 9), and discussed by Campbell and Neubert elsewhere in the present volume. He begins by carefully examining these criteria as "metaperspectives" and concludes that there are some important omissions in Dewey's discussion of both criteria. For instance, Dewey did not adequately comprehend such differences as culture, class, race, and gender. Perhaps for that reason, he fails to fully appreciate the play of power structures in creating and preserving difference in ways that often are oppressive and alienating. Further, Reich realizes, our postmodern situation, characterized by Zygmunt Bauman, for instance, is more ambivalent about notions of social progress than was Dewey. In addition, the problem of enabling democratic assent and dissent without violence and conflict has proven much more intractable than Dewey anticipated, something Campbell and Green seem willing to concede. Although they require considerable rethinking and updating, Reich believes Dewey's metaperspectival criteria remain valuable norms for the democratic practice of education. He focuses on two main lines of reconstruction. First, from the constructivist perspective, Reich proposes an expansion toward an "observer's theory." Distinguishing among the perspectives of "observer," "participant," and "agent" is crucial to the development of Interactive Constructivism. After considering their independent characteristics, and equally importantly their interdependence, he shows that we need an "observer theory" to fully clarify how "facts" are always constructs within the cultural context of observers. Comparing Dewey's and Pierre Bourdieu's construction of the role of scholarly experts in the determination of knowledge indicates, according to Reich, that Dewey's view was too simplistic and optimistic and requires further refinement. Reich's second line of reconstruction suggests that we should emphasize "learning" as a third criterion for democracy. Although Dewey had already attributed a crucial position to learning in the relationship between democracy and education, Reich thinks the time has come for an explicit affirmation of this as a determining criterion for the status of all democratic communities. Interactive Constructivism emphasizes that democratic learning must never confine itself to one interpretive community. Instead, it must expose itself to many interacting communities of interpretation, imagination, communication, observation, and such. He then examines how this three-tiered system could fulfill the original goals of Dewey's criteria while rendering them more useful for dealing with issues of diversity, difference, and power. Reich concludes with a critical observation of the German school system, which does not adequately further democracy.

Continuing the use of Köln Interactive Constructivism to recontextualize and reconstruct Dewey, Neubert's chapter, "Dewey's Pluralism Reconsidered—Pragmatist and Constructivist Perspectives on Diversity and Difference," focuses on questions of diversity and difference. Finding a great deal of value in Dewey's pluralism, Neubert nonetheless asks: What use can we, today, make of Dewey's philosophical pluralism in light of the cultural and philosophical changes that distinguish our own situation from his? He suggests three especially promising lines of critical and creative reconstruction that can help contemporary Deweyans alleviate their own problems in a productive way. These lines concern three central and closely related issues. First, what is the meaning of social progress, and are scientific methods sufficient to secure it? Dewey's social meliorism is not a typical twentieth-century narrative of progress; still, from the perspective of Köln Interactive Constructivism, it is perhaps better to reinterpret Deweyan reconstruction as a never-ending cycle of construction, deconstruction, and reconstruction carried out among many diverse methods interacting with one another (e.g., artistic methods, therapeutic methods, educational methods, and so on). Second, what forms of social control are appropriate for the regulation of social interactions? Sometimes Dewey seems to have excessive confidence in "social engineering" and mechanistic methods that cannot stand up to the challenges of today's globalized, postmodern, postindustrial situation. Köln constructivism recommends an approach expressed in terms of three metaperspectives. The first distinguishes three different relations to a given context, that of the "observer," "participant," and "agent." These relations can be distinguished but interact so intimately that they cannot exist separately. The second distinguishes interaction of "self-observers" with "distant-observers," while the last concerns the interactions of different levels of discourse. The third issue involves the role of difference in democratic conversation. Neubert believes Dewey requires reconstruction because he did not fully recognize the role power relations play in the development of democratic communications. While Dewey's pluralism recognizes difference as being critical to communicative democracy, Neubert contends that he did not adequately understand the role of oppressive power in social relations, including race relations and gender relations. He draws on some of the work done in postcolonial studies to illustrate what is missing. For Neubert, a critical and creative reconstruction must distinguish between those aspects of Dewey's philosophical approach that can best help us rethink the challenges and implications of pluralism for our own time and other aspects of his thought that were characteristic of his time but no longer seem entirely convincing or helpful today.

Hickman's chapter, "Evolutionary Naturalism, Logic, and Lifelong Learning: Three Keys to Dewey's Philosophy of Education," examines the sad state of public discourse in the United States, where its citizenry, its government, and even its academy evidence a serious backlash against what is best termed a scientific or naturalistic worldview. With more confidence in scientific methods than that expressed by Neubert, Hickman examines such antinaturalist positions and utilizes them as foils for a discussion of what he takes to be acceptable forms of naturalism, which are linked by Dewey's well-crafted theory of inquiry to a robust educational philosophy that includes a commitment to programs of lifelong learning. Hickman argues that Dewey's approach is cosmological (and therefore opposed to supernaturalism as accepting the existence of a transcendent deity or deities), yet it is methodologically pluralistic (and therefore opposed to reductive naturalism and materialism). In addition, it is scientific in the sense that it exhibits closure with respect to the space-time causal system that is studied by science. Dewey's naturalism is also *ethical* in the sense that it views norms as arising out of inquiry, which is itself characterized as a natural process, into the means of ameliorating social processes and conditions. Dewey offers a religiously humanistic, but not a secularly humanistic, idea of spirituality. His theory of inquiry is naturalistic in the sense that it arises out of a biological and cultural matrix and returns to those matrices as a part of the orderly process of its work. When inquiry fails to complete this cycle, there is a tendency to vapid abstractions and other forms of irrelevance to human life. Successful inquiry is capable of bridging the putative split between facts and values that has flourished for centuries as philosophical dogma, since it views facts as selected from value-rich contexts and values as open to evaluation by augmented access to facts of a case. At its best, inquiry is a process of lifelong learning. It employs what Dewey calls "genuine" logical concepts, that is, concepts that are constructed as part of a learning process, that exhibit determining principles, and that control their own instances. Such concepts go beyond inductive and nominal abstractions to experimental ones: they are plastic but not arbitrary. Scientific concept formation requires the identification of instances relevant to a problem at hand, the supplementation of those with instances of the same kind, and the location of identified and supplemented instances within a wider conceptual system. As such, genuine scientific concepts afford a naturalistic bulwark against non-naturalistic (including supernaturalistic) alternatives to science and provide platforms for programs of lifelong learning.

Haddock Seigfried's chapter, "Thinking Desire: Taking Perspectives Seriously," focuses on the perspectival character of experience and its consequences for philosophical reflection. She draws on the work not only of Dewey but also of Charles Sanders Peirce, William James, and Jane Addams. She meticulously examines the way that feelings, emotions, and desires influence our apprehensions of reality, that is, the context set by selective interests. Haddock Seigfried believes emotions both help and hinder communication and understanding, and that any adequate explanation of objectivity or values must properly consider them. Unless we respect the noncognitive experience of being, having, and desiring, we will never understand the broader context of knowing. Inquiry is never pure, passionless cognition, because as embodied human beings, we are "thinking desire." Whenever we think, we think about what we need and desire, even if we desire to prove an abstract logical theorem with clarity and coherence. She argues that the flourishing of feminist, black, and multicultural perspective-based philosophies confirms the original pragmatic insights into the importance of personal and collective desire and selective interest. We are perhaps more our emotions than we are ever our thoughts. She gives Deweyan pluralism an embodied and emotional component often ignored in the discussions about difference and diversity. Since the unfairness of partial perspectives is undesirable, many attempt to eliminate them. Haddock Seigfried argues, however, that we cannot eliminate partial perspectives, so it is better to explore various ways of either learning how to combine a plurality of perspectives into a useful unity or mitigate potentially negative effects. Relying on the feminist perspectives of Jane Addams, she expands and reconstructs Dewey's "anti-essentialist," nonreductive, evolving, and feminist-friendly theories of communication and inquiry. She illustrates the force for both positive and negative outcomes of emotionally pervaded perspectives by looking at the response of the U.S. government to terrorism.

Moving in the same direction as Haddock Seigfried, Garrison's, "A Pragmatist Approach to Emotional Expression, Gender, and Identity" examines dominant sociocultural interpretations of emotional expression for clues to the construction of social identity, particularly gender identity. While each chapter in this book discusses the role of habits in Dewey's philosophy, Garrison explicitly explores how cultural norms inscribe themselves as embodied habits that condition an individual's social performance. He supplements Shannon Sullivan's reconstruction of Dewey's theory of habits and Judith Butler's notion of how cultural norms establish scripts of gender "performativity" with some of his own work on Dewey's theory of emotions and emotional interpretation. Garrison concentrates on what is right, and wrong, with Paul Ekman's cross-cultural studies of automatic "affect program" responses and socioculturally mediated "display rules" that override or mask affect response programs. He examines a failed instance of cross-gender communication in a school setting in the United States that involves what Sue Campbell calls "being dismissed" emotionally and what this means for female gender construction. He also mentions an example of social class norms leading to the dismissal of an emotional response to racism. In both instances, he considers the capacity of social power to police social norms. Garrison concludes with a discussion of Dewey's idea that creative, imaginative intelligence, not free will, is the key to freedom. Until we become reflectively aware of our feelings and habits of response and inquire into their sources and destinations, they control us instead of us controlling them. He locates an omission in Dewey's notion of freedom, which sometimes fails to recognize the importance of material conditions in the exercise of intelligence. Garrison calls attention to the affective aspect of communicative democracy by illustrating what can go wrong in dialogues across differences.

In "Moral Norms and Social Inquiry," Hans Seigfried discusses Dewey's efforts to carry over the essential elements of experimental knowing to everyday social experience. The chapter begins with a discussion of Dewey's general pattern of inquiry where, by intelligent action, we arrive at "warranted assertions" that allow us to transform unsettled existential situations to successfully resolve the conflict. Seigfried calls attention to the operational nature not only of ideas but of facts as well, though he, like Hickman, concentrates on the former. The focus is on experimental-operational rules, axioms, and "stable and productive" formal leading principles in Dewey's instrumental theory of inquiry. He especially seeks to emphasize the role of the "pragmatic a priori" in an effort to justify acts of what he calls "logical legislation," by which he mean rules, axioms, and such used as normative guides to further inquiry. Such legislation is practical and not metaphysical or epistemological. The adequacy of an *a priori* principle (i.e., a logical form) to guide future inquiry is only derived from its past successes and, hence, is always subject to falsification and reconstruction. The second part of Seigfried's chapter reviews the use of leading principles in the domain of social inquiry, which serves to expand the scope of application and provide additional tests of the validity of putative guiding principles. Dewey felt that social inquiries lagged behind physical and biological inquiry, not only because of their greater complexity, but even more so because they have not developed their own principles of "logical legislation." Seigfried argues that the idea of operationally *a priori* principles is a more solid basis for social hope than the popular belief that the acceptance of fixed or transcendent universal moral norms in all areas, especially in advanced research and technology, will help us solve our most serious social, moral, and political conflicts. Such assumptions lead to the mistake of thinking social problems are already definitely understood in terms of the customary morality of the society, rather than realizing that they are problems, like other problems, that we may subject to critical reflection and experimental inquiry. Dewey thought that we should refrain from automatically casting social problems as moral problems. Nonetheless, he did not think there were facts independent of our values, moral or otherwise. We should seek to logically legislate the intelligent use of pragmatically *a priori* principles in all domains of human action. Each chapter here refers to Dewey's theory of inquiry. By doing for the role of moral concepts in inquiry what Hickman's chapter does for scientific concepts, Seigfried's contribution brings this book to a well-rounded conclusion.

The chapters here show a smooth progression from the exposition of well-known and popular themes in Dewey's work, such as pluralistic democracy and scientific inquiry, through a reconstruction of these themes, to the emphases on themes such as the inclusion of emotions clearly present in Dewey, though infrequently critically explored. All along the way, Dewey is challenged, revised, recontextualized, and updated in ways that should intrigue readers interested in the status of Dewey scholarship today.

Notes

1. References to the writings of Dewey are to the critical edition, *The Collected Works of John Dewey*, 1967–1972, 1976–1983, 1981–1983, ed. Jo Ann Boydston (Carbondale: Southern Illinois University Press). Abbreviations for the critical edition are as follows:

EW   *The Early Works* (1882–1898)
MW   *The Middle Works* (1899–1924)
LW   *The Later Works* (1925–1953)

The volume number and page number follow the initials of the series.

2. Chapter 3 of Dewey's *Individualism, Old and New* (LW 5) is titled: "The United States, Incorporated." Today, "Corporate America" is a global idea associated with companies such as IBM, Exxon, and R. J. Reynolds. Much of what defines globalism is a culture of greed; often it is the continuation of nationalist colonialism by other means.

Works Cited

Rockefeller, S. 1991. *John Dewey: Religious faith and democratic humanism*. New York: Columbia University Press.
Norton, A. 2004. *Leo Strauss and the Politics of American Empire*. New Haven: Yale University Press.

Chapter 1

The Political Philosophy
of Pragmatism

James Campbell

This chapter is a two-part discussion of the political philosophy of pragmatism and its implications for today.
First, as an explanation of the political philosophy of pragmatism, I offer a reconsideration of the key themes in John
Dewey's 1927 volume, *The Public and Its Problems* (LW 2).
Second, as a consideration of the contemporary implications of
pragmatic social thought, I offer a discussion of the current
state of American community.

I begin with the reminder that America has always been a culture of communities. Whether Americans focus on early religious
groups such as the Pilgrims and Puritans, or on more temporary
groups such as the members of wagon trains and residents of slave
quarters, or on native tribes or immigrant ghettoes, the American
story has always been one of groups of people and their shared
lives. Americans may talk incessantly about liberties and rights and
freedoms but, fortunately, their lives do not match their privatistic
rhetoric. Without a strong context of community, such individualism would have caused American society to unwind long ago.

I

One of the essential texts in American social thought is Dewey's volume *The Public and Its Problems*. The central value of this volume is that in it Dewey puts the focus of political thinking on community and communities, which he calls "publics." I would like to emphasize six themes from this volume. The first is that as a historical event, *The Public and Its Problems* appeared in 1927 in a context of grave doubts about the possibilities of American democracy. The negative factors were numerous. There was the almost-universal support for, and later repudiation of, World War I. There was the postwar Red Scare and the enactment of Prohibition. Doubts about the wisdom of these public policies were enhanced by claims about the deficient IQs of American military recruits (and, by implication, of other citizens). The final straw was perhaps the anti-intellectual legislation that led to the Scopes Trial in July 1925. As a result of these democratic "failures," there was a strong feeling that democracy could not deal with the complex problems of modern living. In Europe, this distrust of democracy was being felt in the initial stirrings of Fascism. In America, the anti-democratic response was inclined more toward technocracy.

One of the American anti-democrats was Walter Lippmann, who suggested that matters of political concern had become *expert* matters, dealings with sewage and hospitals and electricity and fire protection, about which average citizens did not know enough to decide wisely. Unfortunately, he continued, the American political system is based on the assumption that its citizens are "omnicompetent." Lippmann's solution was to have the people stand aside and let the experts do their jobs, intervening only at certain critical times (e.g., elections) to remove those who are not getting the work of government done. Another way to phrase this point is that, for Lippmann, good government is possible only if we give up self-government. In response to this technocratic criticism, Dewey's overall aim in *The Public and Its Problems* is to reject the assertion that democracy had failed and to propose, on the contrary, that America needed a fuller and richer democracy.

Dewey's second point is the primacy of the community (public) over the individual in public life. He indicates this primacy when he discusses interactions:

> Sometimes the consequences [of our actions] are confined to those who directly share in the transaction which produces them. In other cases they extend far beyond those immediately engaged in producing them. Thus two kinds of interests...are generated. In the first, [they] are limited to those directly engaged; in the second, they extend to those who do not directly share in the performance of acts. If, then, the interest constituted by their being affected by the actions in question is to have any practical influence, control over the actions which produce them must occur by some indirect means. (LW 2: 257)

From this communal concern with indirect consequences "a public" and eventually a government arise. As Dewey continues, "[T]he public consists of all those who are affected by the indirect consequences of transactions to such an extent that it is deemed necessary to have those consequences systematically cared for. Officials are those who look out for and take care of the interests thus affected" (245–46).

Dewey's second theme in *The Public and Its Problems* is thus that when an individual or a group of individuals performs actions that have an impact on others, those others, that is, the public, have a right to protect themselves.

Dewey's third point is the need for an open or a pragmatic understanding of the state. He tells us that the only possible definition of the state is "a purely formal one: The state is the organization of the public effected through officials for the protection of the interests shared by its members" (256). He does eventually suggest that we can be a bit more specific, and he offers what he calls four "marks" of a state.

The first is that a state is found somewhere between a face-to-face community, where there are lots of common interests but few indirect results, and more or less isolated regions, where there are no common interests.

The second is that the community comes, over time, to be concerned with certain kinds of results and to want some level of uniformity and security with situations that recur. In other words, as we move from place to place and from context to context, we want to be able to trust our food and our roads, our airplanes and our insurance policies. This trust is established when the community puts its collective security in the hands of its government.

The third is that the community recognizes that there are those who cannot get by on their own, and who thus need to be protected. Some of these dependencies are temporary, as in the case of children; others are more permanent, as in the case of the disabled. Dewey's general principle here is: "When the parties involved in any transaction are unequal in status, the relationship is likely to be one-sided, and the interests of one party to suffer" (274). In such transactions, we use our government as a protector of last-resort.

The fourth is that the community is to judge when the scope of the indirect results merits communal control. Over time, the community can change its mind. As a result, for example, concerns with religion and most other intellectual matters have moved from the *public* to the *private* sphere at the same time the professional lives of physicians and others have fallen under public regulation. Where the line is to be drawn remains, for Dewey, a social decision. Dewey's third point in *The Public and Its Problems*, then, is that our understanding of the state should be an open or a pragmatic one.

Dewey's fourth main point in this book is the evolutionary theme of the importance of defending this flexibility in our communal actions. Because the government is defined primarily through its adaptive *function* rather than through some (presumed) *essence*, the scope of its efforts will change over the years. At times, the responsibilities of the government will be expanding and at other times contracting. The only possible answer to the question of how big the government should be is: as big as it has to be. Similarly, there is no final answer to the question of whether the community should be involved with providing or subsidizing any of the following: education through the university level, health care, public transportation, utilities, and retirement. Whether the community should be so engaged is a matter for its members to decide, and, while Americans seem to be in a minimalist mood at present, there is no finality to this

phase. (This theme of the importance of flexibility in government is closely connected to the discussions of the nature of
inquiry in the chapters by Hickman and Hans Seigfried.)

Dewey presents this evolutionary theme in three related
versions. The first, which we can call the "philosophical version," we have just seen: The government should be whatever
size and shape it needs to be in order to get the public's work
done. The second version of this theme is more "historical" in
nature. Here, Dewey's point is that Americans' understanding
of democracy was scarred as a result of the historical conditions
present when it was being developed. "Born in revolt against
established forms of government and the state," he writes, "the
events which finally culminated in democratic political forms
were deeply tinged by fear of government, and were actuated
by a desire to reduce it to a minimum so as to limit the evil it
could do" (288–89). Limitations on the range of democracy
that began in our initial context, when they may have made
good sense, have unfortunately been imported into our very
different situations as precedent. Dewey's third version of this
evolutionary theme is a more "political" one. The result of this
limited conception of government in 1927 was that Americans
have a country that is becoming less and less democratic, a
place where citizens are decreasingly likely to have a say in
what matters in their lives. As the economy became central-
ized, figures with power used these limitations on democracy
to hamper the community's ability to restrain them. From
these three versions, we recognize the importance of Dewey's
point, that we understand the government as an adaptive tool
for solving our problems.

Given all that we have seen, Dewey's next point would have
to be the necessity for changes, and he calls in *The Public and Its
Problems*, and in his other political writings, for deliberate *intellectual* and *institutional* reconstruction. The intellectual reconstruction would entail developing new ways of thinking about
our shared lives. One such change that he advocated was that
we come to see democracy as a way of life rather than as a
narrow political system. Another was that we come to see community as a moral association. Dewey's ideas on institutional
reconstruction presented new ways for Americans to organize

their shared lives, ways designed not to replace democracy but to make it work again.

One change was to foster social inquiry, based upon his belief that it is necessary to find out by deliberate effort what the problems of our society are. We need to abandon our acceptance of traditional answers and adopt more systematized inquiry into such questions as how medical care is best provided or how teenage pregnancy is to be minimized. (As might be expected, all of the chapters in this book consider the theme of social inquiry.) A second institutional change was that we need to further the communication of this information. Without better dissemination, citizens will continue to make poor and harmful decisions. Dewey is of the opinion that our failure to communicate this knowledge is not the result of inadequate means, or the stupidity or apathy of the populace, but the result of our misunderstanding of the nature of ideas and knowledge as private property. For Dewey, on the contrary, we are fundamentally social beings: "We are born organic beings associated with others, but we are not born members of a community.... To learn to be human is to develop through the give-and-take of communication an effective sense of being an individually distinctive member of a community." (331–32). He believes that by working and solving problems together, by interacting with others with similar interests, and so on, individuals will come to recognize their interdependence, develop respect for their fellows, and build community. Thus for Dewey political activity is a kind of educational experience, and its method is cooperative inquiry. It is necessary for our educational institutions to both introduce the young into the shared values of their society and to give them some distance from their common life. In a democracy, education must prepare the young for their lives as future citizens. It must be moral, not just intellectual; emphasize judgment, rather than just skills of calculating; aim at wisdom, rather than just knowledge; and foster cooperation, rather than "getting ahead." Dewey's fifth point in *The Public and Its Problems* is a call for intellectual and institutional reconstruction to make our democratic practice more like cooperative inquiry.

Dewey's final point in this volume is the importance of faith in the possibilities of democratic community. On the one hand, community remains of central importance to us, because our collective problems provide us with a self-conscious directing force. As Dewey puts it, "[U]nless local communal life can be restored, the public cannot adequately resolve its most urgent problem: to find and identify itself" (370). On the other hand, community satisfies a deep psychological need: "There is something deep within human nature itself which pulls toward settled relationships.... That happiness which is full of content and peace is found only in enduring ties with others, which reach to such depths that they go below the surface of conscious experience to form its undisturbed foundation" (368). Dewey's belief is, ultimately, that we must have faith in our fellows for democracy to work.

II

After this consideration of various aspects of community in pragmatic philosophy, what might we say about the present situation in America?[1] American society is deeply divided. Its members are suspicious of, and hostile toward, each other. American community, it seems, is broken. While there are perhaps any number of ways to try to approach the core of these troubles, I will attempt to do so by concentrating on what I think are the four central aspects.

The first of these is the assumption on the part of many American politicians and their supporters that there is only one solution to any of our problems, and that they are in possession of this solution. In any intellectual endeavor, of course, such bankrupt *absolutism* would be rejected immediately. In a similar fashion, absolutism has no place in cooperative social inquiry; but as we all know, it functions quite successfully in contemporary politics. A second aspect of the contemporary American situation is the often-unasserted assumption that any political position should be articulable in a small number of categorical sentences, preferably one. Some political positions, as we know, demonstrate this sort of *oversimplification*—this group is our enemy, that country is our friend—but surely this quality alone does not make them good positions. Our contemporary situation calls for cooperative deliberation leading toward circumspect action, but a large number of our politicians, and an alarming number of our citizens, view nuance as obfuscation and subtlety as a sign of weakness.

Rather than engaging in the sort of cooperative inquiry that respects a plurality of opinions and assumes the complexity of social problems, the American climate of absolutism and oversimplification attacks those who do not share our simple creed as being "bad" Americans. Our politicians use *partisanship* as a divisive tool to "energize the troops" through hatred of the "enemy." They deliberately focus upon issues such as the war, abortion, homosexuality, and religion in public life to foster divisiveness within the society. In their terms, they try to "drive a wedge" through the electorate. Finally, this cluster of absolutism, oversimplification, and partisanship is sealed off from a major source of criticism by Americans' *chauvinism*, our exaggerated patriotism that makes us suspicious of all outsiders. We find ourselves at present in a climate where no "foreign" evaluations of what we do, whether it be continuing inappropriate executions or driving wasteful vehicles or waging preemptive war, need be considered, because those who offer such criticisms are, by definition, not Americans. The American self-image has long included the assumption that we are different from, and probably better than, other peoples. Some level of collective self-satisfaction may, in fact, be necessary for social stability; and no doubt Russians and Filipinos and Saudis and Germans have some of their own problems with chauvinism. Americans seem at present, however, uncontrolled in our rejection of whatever is not "American"; and our excessive self-regard borders on hatred of foreigners. In our misguided attempt to "strengthen" America, we have forgotten the fundamental message of Dewey, that a society has an inside and an outside. As he noted, there are two criteria for evaluating any social group. The first is internal, its level of shared interests; the second is external, its interaction and cooperation with other groups. As he wrote, we need to ask: "How numerous and varied are the interests which are consciously shared? How full and free is the interplay with other forms of association?" (MW 9: 89).[2] (These two criteria are discussed further by Reich and Neubert in their chapters.) Americans, on the other hand, seem to be trying to build a strong society by turning within.

Collectively, these four factors make contemporary American politics a mess. For me, this mess is a serious problem, and one that we cannot solve until we recognize its source in our weakened community. Additionally, in all four of the aspects to which I have pointed, I have suggested that American politicians have failed; but we all know that the situation is more complex, and that the solution must come from the people. No absolutizing candidate or officeholder could ever succeed if citizens did not fall for such pronouncements, and no oversimplified rationale would ever be presented if better analyses were demanded. The solution to America's current problems is not just to get different politicians. If it is to come at all, the solution will have to come from the American people, by forming themselves into better communities.

Given this gloom, what possibilities are there for pragmatic social thought to contribute to reconciliation? Solving this present impasse will mean working to reestablish community. One aspect of the effort to recover community is for Americans to learn to work with those whose ideas they reject and whose policies they oppose. To move out of their current fragmented state, Americans may even need to compromise on issues they regard as uncompromisable, and to abandon values they regard as unabandonable. The question is: How might reconciliation be possible? Let us consider one model from America's collective past. A little over 140 years ago, on March 4, 1865, Abraham Lincoln offered his Second Inaugural Address. Speaking during the final phase of the Civil War, he was a drained man, working within an America that was far more divided than it is now. Even so, he thought that reconciliation was possible. In his address, Lincoln phrased his intention as follows: "With malice toward none; with charity for all; with firmness in the right, as God gives us to see the right, let us strive on to finish the work we are in; to bind up the nation's wounds... to do all which may achieve and cherish a just, and a lasting peace" (Lincoln [1865] 1953, 8: 333). Perhaps there is something we can learn from Lincoln's approach to reconciliation for our time.

The most noticeable aspect of this address, just hinted at in the passage I quoted, is its deeply religious tone. (Green discusses other aspects of Americans' religiosity in her chapter.) After enduring the unending horror of his first presidency, Lincoln was able to interpret this great tragedy only in religious terms. Both parties, he notes, "read the same Bible, and pray to the same God"; each side "invokes His aid against the other." After four years of slaughter, Lincoln maintains that neither side could claim that its prayers had been "answered fully." His interpretation for the indecisive struggle is not divine indifference, however, but that "[t]he Almighty has his own purposes." For Lincoln, it seems, the slaughter was too much for humans to understand; all that we could do is accept the mystery and struggle on as God gives us to see the right. "Fondly do we hope , fervently do we pray, that this mighty scourge of war may speedily pass away," he writes, "Yet, if God wills that it continue . . . so still it must be said, the judgments of the Lord, are true and righteous altogether" (8: 333).

Could Lincoln's approach to reconciling the two sides of his deeply split state be of any use to us now? For starters, his final theme of resignation would not seem very helpful. Perhaps there is more to be gained from emphasizing other aspects of Lincoln's position. Is there an aspect that is more pragmatic? How about adopting Lincoln's fallibilism? By his fallibilism, Lincoln attempted to place both sides in the Civil War on less certain moral footing. Even on the seemingly unambiguous question of slavery itself, "wringing their bread from the sweat of other men's faces," fallible Lincoln's view was "let us judge not that we be not judged" (8: 333). Could Americans perhaps follow him here and step back from any strongly held positions to allow for more flexibility in their stances? Could they admit, for example, that they might be wrong about some of the central issues that they are defending? If abortion or homosexuality were no longer matters of dispute, then the American community would presumably be much less divided; and, if their squabbles over the war or over the role of religion in public life were resolved, then the Americans could presumably turn to rebuilding the community. On these issues, as on all others, humans are fallible; and they might recognize at some later point that they were wrong. Americans could no doubt make such concessions in favor of reconciliation as a Lincolnian higher good, but should they do this? Two things seem to hold them back. The first is that since their opponents are equally fallible, they could yield instead. The second restraint is that these beliefs are not just "beliefs"; in part, beliefs constitute who we are. Americans are part of a group, or better a number of groups, with deeply felt positions on abortion, homosexuality, the war, and the role of religion in public life. These values have a particular and powerful meaning and are not something to be compromised away.

As I indicated earlier, for me there is too much religion in Lincoln's approach to communal reconciliation. (Of course, as Hickman points out in his chapter, my opponent here should not be religion, but supernatural religion.) But perhaps there is something in Lincoln's underlying stance of fallibilism as a tool for movement toward reconciliation. One means of reconciliation, then, would seem to be to adjust moral claims about social policies. The way to deal with those Americans' claims that are increasingly absolutistic, oversimplified, partisan, and chauvinistic might be to adopt claims that are tentative, nuanced, and open-minded, that is, pragmatic. It will surely be tough to compromise with opponents whose values are so different. It is, moreover, difficult to imagine these opponents ready to compromise, and any "weakness" on the pragmatists' part might amount to surrender. Difficult or not, however, communal reconciliation may be possible. Or it may be that communal reconciliation is simply not possible under current American circumstances. Perhaps the process of cooperative interaction to rebuild a larger community is not the higher good now. Perhaps preserving the more open values of the smaller community is. Perhaps the job of pragmatism is to hold them off until they destruct in an eventual fireball of their own self-righteousness. This stance assumes, of course, that pragmatists will be able to survive that catastrophe and then take up the difficult task of reconstructing America's fragmented society. I am willing to make that assumption. I still believe that America will somehow right itself, but I must reluctantly admit that I do not see this happening soon.

It would seem, then, that the current state of American political life indicates little regard for Dewey's pragmatic message. In part, his call for an open understanding of the role of the state has been rejected by those whose fixed and narrow interpretation is rooted in their sense of its historical role. In part, his call for extensive changes in our democratic thought and practices has encountered the response that our traditional ways of thinking and acting are just fine. And, in part, Dewey's call for faith in the possibilities of democracy to solve our social problems through cooperative inquiry has been met with partisan arrogance by those who see no value in cooperation. This current state is, of course, transitional. Another part of Dewey's message of faith in democracy is that the people will eventually awaken.

Notes

1. This section draws upon my essay, "Community, Conflict, and Reconciliation."

2. Cf. Dewey: "A member of a robber band may express his powers in a way consonant with belonging to that group and be directed by the interest common to its members. But he does so only at the cost of repression of those of his potentialities which can be realized only through membership in other groups" (LW 2: 328).

Works Cited

Campbell, J. 2005. Community, conflict and reconciliation. *Journal of Speculative Philosophy* 19: 4, 187–200.

Lincoln, A. [1865] 1953. Second Inaugural Address. In *The collected works of Abraham Lincoln*, ed. Roy P. Basler, 8: 332–333. 8 vols. New Brunswick, NJ: Rutgers University Press.

Lippmann, W. [1922] 1965. *Public opinion*. New York: Free Press.

Chapter 2

Dr. Dewey's Deeply Democratic Metaphysical Therapeutic for the Post-9/11 American Democratic Disease

Toward Cultural Revitalization and Political Reinhabitation

Judith Green

Given a world like that in which we live, a world in which environing changes are partly favorable and partly callously indifferent,...any control attainable by the living creature depends upon what is done to alter the state of things. Success and failure are the primary "categories" of life: achieving of good and averting of ill are its supreme interests; hope and anxiety (which are not self-enclosed states of feeling, but active attitudes of welcome and wariness) are dominant qualities of experience.

— John Dewey, "The Need for a Recovery of Philosophy"

The cure for the ailments of democracy is more democracy.
— John Dewey, *The Public and Its Problems.*

Introduction: America's Post-9/11 Anxiety and Longing for Democratic Hope

Shared social hope has been a life-and-death matter for the American people since September 11, 2001 (hereafter 9/11), because we now live with a shared, deep anxiety from which no level of privilege can save us, in a "homeland" that never again will feel truly secure. What we long for is authentic, shared existential hope for an open, democratic future, grounded in the kind of unity in fellow feeling we Americans briefly experienced with one another and with countless other world citizens for a few weeks after that dreadful day when terrorists brought down New York City's Twin Towers and destroyed many more lives than those they took in those twin holocausts. As individuals and as a people, we long to believe again that democracy is the source of America's strength—not military might, not the catbird seat in global capitalism, not the kind of totalitarian nationalism that spies on its own citizens, demands their uncritical obedience, and justifies the torture and demonization of other cultures as the necessary price of self-preservation. We long to raise the proud banner of the democratic ideal once again, and we long to feel that we are part of a progressive current in history. In an always uncertain world of human experience, we long to frame events in terms of the better possibilities toward which we aspire, to give our best energies to shared efforts to actualize these ideals, and to learn, to grow, to find meaning, and to experience sufficient success in these efforts to keep alive the life-directing dream of democracy for ourselves, for citizens of other nations, and for all of our children's children.

Such shared democratic hope is difficult for us now, however, not only because of 9/11 but even more because of its active frustration by anti-democratic currents in our American political processes and within our multicultural streams of daily living during the months and years that have followed 9/11. Campbell has described eloquently how America's always-differing regional, religious, ethnic, and political groups have become very suspicious of one another in recent years, their distrust fanned by politicians who have employed anti-democratic tactics of absolutism, oversimplification, partisanship, and chauvinism. I would add, however, that these have been specifically neoconservative tactics employed by our president's party to enhance their ability to exercise "emergency powers" against enemies they claim are inside as well as outside our nation. Rival politicians have found it difficult to counter such tactics, because the kind of alternative analysis of our problem situation we need now is difficult to frame in a few words as a "sound bite." In addition, they have been shocked at their fellow Americans' gullibility and willingness to give up hard-won democratic rights in order to support exercises of presidential power that clearly have made our situation in the world and our relations with each other worse rather than better. As Reich rightly argues, relational power has been at stake in recent cultural and political struggles over how much democracy is feasible in the twenty-first century. For those whose answer is "very little," the next question becomes: *whose* power will triumph in struggles among the nations and among the diverse cultures, religions, races, genders, economic groups, and regions that now make up American society?

"Hope deferred makes the heart sick," Proverbs tells us, and we as an American people are sick at heart now because our actuality is drifting so far off the course guided by the beloved possibilities expressed within our long-shared democratic ideal. Vague though it may be, this American dream-ideal expresses some of the kinds of desires that run deep and powerful in us, as Haddock Seigfried rightly reminds. Though we express our shared dream in local tongues, the "inner" power of this dream-ideal links Americans inseparably amidst our "outer" power-structured differences, even when we deny it in our words and actions, making us restless and dissatisfied with ourselves even when we seem clearly determined to refuse Garrison's wise and necessary call to dialogue across differences. Our American dream-sickness is now so acute and so deep that we cannot seem to agree about what ails us and how to remedy it. In fact, interpretive differences concerning our post-9/11 problem situation have become so great that our allegiances to rival background stories or "big pictures" have divided the American people

- into "red states" and "blue states";
- into fierce proponents of the Iraq War and those who are nauseated by it;
- into those who think religion is the source of our problem, and those who see it as our salvation;
- into those who see growing economic inequality as a sign of global capitalism's success, and those who see it as a sign of its failure;
- into those who advocate student-centered multicultural education, and those who demand an accountable, uniform national curriculum;
- into those who see reassertion of cultural and legal control over women's bodies as the rightful responsibility of our churches, our universities, and our courts, and those who are prepared to stake their futures on resisting such patriarchal domination;
- into those who have already forgotten the thousands of dead black bodies and the countless tearful black survivors of Hurricane Katrina—or even regard the incalculable devastation of New Orleans as God's judgment on this American Gomorrah—and those who regard the abject, racialized poverty Katrina revealed, as well as our nation's refusal or inability to care for our own fellow citizens, as history's judgment on American democracy; and
- into those who still reach out in hospitality to newcomers from faraway places, and those who see only potential terrorists, "wetbacks," and new claimants on our war-impoverished public coffers.

John Dewey and Richard Rorty offer us very different kinds of advice about how to address this post-9/11 American problem situation. Dewey advised us to employ all of the philosophical tools we have inherited while reconstructing them as needed to guide and to express the results of a focused, intelligent, cooperative social inquiry that seeks deep democratic transformations. In contrast, Rorty advised us to give up philosophy as earlier understood in order to tell a "new American story" as convincingly as we can, and to make common cause with labor leaders in limited campaigns of reform that seek to "achieve our country" by working for fuller economic justice within America's existing institutional constraints of a liberal constitution and a capitalist economy. While both Dewey and Rorty valorize democracy and individuality, and both reject a dualistic substance metaphysics, and both propose alternatives to the old correspondence theory of truth and the "spectator" theory of knowledge, what they mean when they use what at first may seem to be a common vocabulary is totally different. In fact, their difference over whether to "do" metaphysics in any recognizable sense is symptomatic of a whole pattern of differences in philosophical practice between them that requires us to choose between their rival "pragmatist" and "neopragmatist" systems of curing in our search for post-9/11 cultural and political healing.[1] They both could be wrong, but they cannot both be right.

Which philosophical model—if either—can offer us helpful advice about how to address the deep anxieties, profound longings, and event-shaping moods and emotions that actively influence our dynamically emerging and changing individual and communal worldviews, as well as the national and international policies that our formal democratic system now expresses, impresses, and reflects back into them? How can we get a handle on which—if any—of the worldviews currently contending in the public square, in our hearts and minds, and in our practices of daily living more adequately engages the realities of our times; which clarifies the cultural and potential alternatives before us; which helps us most effectively to recognize those world-changing choices we may have, and to make the better choices?

My answer here is this: Dewey's curing system all the way, including his pragmatist method of inquiry and his "low-rise" process metaphysic that focuses on our feeling-saturated human role in recognizing and delineating events, on generic and enduring traits of experience, and on therapeutic processes of analysis, communication, and democratic social transformation. In my earlier work, I distinguished two meanings and levels of democracy: The formal or institutional level, and the "deep" level of habits, practices, attitudes, and hopes in daily living. I now see the need to distinguish a third, metaphysical "background" level of dynamic, emotion-encompassing, experience-framing democratic vision as an object of reflection and as a life-guiding tool for influencing the development of democracy at the other two levels. So understood, this democratic background vision is what Dewey—writing in an era before the wider presence of women as philosophers he longed for led to more inclusive turns of language than his own—referred to as a "metaphysic of the common man." I believe its effective employment is necessary within any comprehensive cure to the "democratic disease" that now ails the American people. Please let me explain.

In *Deep Democracy: Community, Diversity, and Transformation* (Green 1999), I argued that formal, institutional democracies are not sustainable, and may not even be desirable, unless they are grounded in and challenged by more deeply democratic institutions, customs, values, and habits of everyday living. In the absence of such a deep democracy, or in conditions of its erosion, even "experienced democracies" such as the United States fall prey to what I have called the fourfold "democratic disease"—institutional subvertibility, ideological hollowness, individual nihilism, and cultural anomie—that is now so common in the West.[2] Since 9/11, the scope of this "democratic disease" has grown to such epidemic proportions in America that it has been possible for George W. Bush to convince a narrow majority of the American people to surrender many of their hard-won civil rights, to oppose the full extension of these rights to gays and lesbians, and to pursue an open-ended "war against terrorism" that already has involved invading two other nations in the name of American patriotism and "homeland security." We Americans are a people in desperate need of healing from this fourfold "democratic disease," for our own sake as well as that of the community of nations within which we now wield shockingly anti-democratic powers. Dewey recommended a course of cultural and political therapy that I believe is precisely what the American people need today: "The cure for the ailments of democracy is more democracy." For American philosophers today and our consulting practitioners in other countries, our challenge as contemporary diagnosticians and therapists is to discover what Dewey's wise directive means for us now, after 9/11, as we project a course of treatment for America's now-dangerous stage of the democratic disease. In the last chapter of *Deep Democracy*, I outlined nine general aspects of fully actualized deep democracies and six predictably recurring stages within collaborative democratic transformation projects that aim to rebuild "the public square" in more deeply democratic ways. My project here is to focus on the question of how to more fully actualize two of these aspects of deep democracy—democratic cultural revitalization and political reinhabitation—in the context of America's problematic cultural and political situation since 9/11, with an awareness that such transformations would have great significance for other nations as well.

In working up a course of transformative treatment that is likely to be effective in our current American problem situation, it will be necessary not only to consider the wider context of globalization that has contributed to the development of America's democratic disease and that complicates its remedy, but also to reckon with the communicative challenge arising from my expectation that my diagnosis will seem to many to be an unsolicited "second opinion" that would require them to fire their old "doctors," to face some hard truths about reality, and to develop some new habits of living. Moreover, my diagnosis and proposed remedy would require many of my philosophical colleagues to undertake a refresher course in Dewey's "metaphysic" in order to reorient their approach to philosophical practice and to update their tools of diagnosis and therapeutic treatment, so as to make these more likely to promote healing and hope. Among those I would invite to such a refresher course in Deweyan "metaphysic" are the late Richard Rorty, Jürgen Habermas, and my pragmatist feminist friend, Charlene Haddock Seigfried, who has argued, not without reason, that we should give up both the term *metaphysics* and the philosophical terrain it traditionally has designated, because these inevitably entangle our energies in struggles over what Dewey called "the problems of philosophers," and thereby distract us from what he called "the problems of men"—the urgent social problems of our times.

However, instead of wasting our time and diverting our energies, I believe such a refresher course in Dewey's "metaphysic"—with appropriate updates—will help us to communicate more effectively with the American "patients" who must again become democratic agents of their own healing and hope. It will help us unmask the quacks who are now having far too much success in selling their outdated nostrums and their radical surgeries to a fearful, anxious, nostalgic, and gullible public. And it will help us engage most effectively with a wider community of knowledgeable thinkers and democratic inquirers across time, across schools of philosophical thought, across disciplines, and across cultures, with whom we must collaborate in manifold ways if we are to save the patients and to prevent this now-epidemic American democratic disease from destroying all hope for a global democratic future.

What's Metaphysics Got to Do With It?

In order to show what Dewey meant by his "metaphysic," and why I think we would be wise to renew it rather than discard it to speed our efforts to foster America's democratic cultural revitalization and political reinhabitation, I contrast the course of treatment I think it guides with the one Rorty proposed only a few years before 9/11. In *Achieving Our Country: Leftist Thought in Twentieth-Century America* (1998a) and in *Philosophy and Social Hope* (1999), Rorty offered a critical diagnosis of what already ailed us Americans at that time. He mapped out a course of treatment that called for "intellectuals" to offer their storytelling services to a "leftist" political vanguard led by labor unions that would organize a campaign to renew America's commitment to economic justice as expressed by a limited agenda of reforms within the framework of America's existing political and economic institutions. I argue here that Rorty's prescription cannot lead us to a more deeply democratic, post-9/11 cultural revitalization and political reinhabitation, but that a different course of diagnosis and therapy suggested and fostered in part by applying Dewey's "metaphysic" can promote healing, growth, and hope for the democratic future of our nation and the world.

In writing *Achieving Our Country*, Rorty seems to have had difficulty making up his mind about whether explaining the meaning and importance of this project to a wide "intellectual" audience requires plunging into the currently unpopular shoals of metaphysics, a cold bath Dewey frequently found helpful in clarifying his vision and never gave up, although it required him to swim against strong currents in Western philosophy and in contemporary political life. On the one hand, arguing against the great twentieth-century liberal philosopher, John Rawls, who famously claimed in a 1985 essay that issues of justice, including the preferability of democratic forms of living, can be understood in purely political terms without metaphysical implications, Rorty quoted Dewey in arguing that the meaning of democracy is not reducible to a set of political forms and processes, because it is ultimately, in some sense, metaphysical: "Democracy is neither a form of government nor a social expediency, but a metaphysic of the relation of man and his experience in nature."[3] On the other hand, Rorty apologetically called Dewey's language of metaphysics in this passage "a bit unfortunate," and he misleadingly suggested that all Dewey meant was that, contra Nietzsche, "democracy is the principal means by which a more evolved form of humanity will come into existence" (1998, 142).

Surprisingly, in spite of this move to lighten the weightiness of a democratic metaphysics, Rorty went on to say, using Kenneth Burke's language, that the human persons who emerge from the kinds of deeply democratic processes of living for which Dewey called will have "more being" than pre-democratic humanity: "The citizens of a democratic, Whitmanesque society are able to create new, hitherto unimagined roles and goals for themselves. So a greater variety of perspectives, and of descriptive terms, becomes available to them, and can with justice be used to account for them" (1999, 143). Rorty's phrase, "with justice," carries a great deal of weight in grounding the application of these so-called "descriptive terms," evoking as it does older metaphysical cords of meaning that suggest a divine perspective, or directive forces within nature, or at least common standards of judgment within a shared tradition. Yet

Rorty explicitly attempts to cut away each kind of metaphysical tethers to the past, leaving only a slim linguistic thread of what it is possible for us to say in a common language that appeals for the liberation of individuals. How such appeals could work and why anyone would or should attend to them are among the things Rorty leaves unsaid.

These are dangerous silences for a democratic "story" that aims to clarify and to revive our shared commitment to "achieving our country" now, because this necessarily requires us to explain ourselves to one another and to those in other global contexts who do not entirely share our "form of life"— or may even be antagonistic toward it—but whose assent or at least tolerance will be necessary if emerging world conditions are to support our hopes for a sustainable peace that will allow us to invest our time and treasure in deepening democracy, instead of in prosecuting wars and defending our "homeland" from international and domestic terrorists. Rorty has left out two key elements in his linguistically "lite" version of democratic metaphysics:

1. how we should understand the process of transforming a culture's internal social relations and transactional practices, which Dewey rightly regarded as inseparable from the liberation of individuals; and
2. how we should understand the characteristic processes that shape and guide transactions among those communities, nations, and international associations that helpfully structure or distort the transactions of individuals with one another and with the larger whole of nature.

In short, Rorty has forgotten the "socialist" dimension of the Progressives' metaphysics that concerns the deep grounding, quality, and equitability of our connections to one another and to the larger whole of nature locally, nationally, and globally. In brief, Dewey and the other Progressives held that an adequate ethics, politics, and economics must be grounded in a realistic, nondualistic, process metaphysics that concurs with and helps guide an adequate physics, biology, social psychology, and theology. Such a background view or "big picture" understands humans as inextricably interconnected to one another and to other living and inorganic entities within local life systems and within the larger whole of nature, from which they emerge and within which they may grow and individuate into particular, active, creative agent-patients who, in turn, influence local and global futures through their ongoing, partially controllable transactions with each other and with their wider world. Thus an ontology that is realistic and useful for world understanding and future guiding must be "socialist" rather than "individualist"—it must reflect these necessary networks of transactional relations that go "all the way down" within our being and becoming. At the same time, it must be "socialist" in recognizing the complex, dynamic interplay of the humanity-constituting elements within our processively individuating social selves—our bodily organs and functions interplaying with our emotions, interplaying with our thinking, interplaying with our experiences of world undergoing and our experiences of active effort and engagement—all of this self-becoming and patient-agent experience always involving profound social influences of other humans as individuals and group members, as well as social influences of our participation in a wider biotic community.

The importance of this "metaphysical" dimension—background visions or "big pictures" that frame basic understandings of reality about which the American people and the wider world are now deeply divided—has become abundantly clear since 9/11. Contrary to Rorty, Rawls, Habermas, Heidegger, and Haddock Seigfried, I believe it is wiser to reengage in Dewey's project of reconstructing such a "socialist" metaphysics, not as a "first philosophy" that can be thought of as somehow "preceding" experience but rather as a therapeutic dimension of reflective thinking about "already had" experience that can spur critical insights about the particular intellectual habits and cultural assumptions that help construct our "uptake" on experience, past and future. In addition to its critical dimension, such a democratic "socialist" metaphysics also may spur transformative insights about how we might think and live differently—better—in our transactions with one another as humans and with the wider natural world in which our lives necessarily take part.

Dewey's Democratic Metaphysical Therapeutics

Dewey often used medical imagery to describe, differentiate, or point toward the proper work of philosophy, even before he published his great pragmatist manifesto, "The Need for a Recovery of Philosophy" (MW 10), and he continued to employ this medical metaphor throughout the great works of his mature years. Words such as "ailment," "remedy," "cure," "recovery," and "instrument" are key elements of Dewey's vocabulary within texts he wrote with the aim of stimulating a reimagination of the work of philosophy that both reclaims and reconstructs the original, ancient visions of its earliest practitioners. This is another example of the insightfulness of Randall's characterization of Dewey as "the greatest traditionalist among the leading philosophical minds of today" who sought to honor and maintain fruitful continuities with rich, earlier traditions, even as he sought to reorient and revitalize philosophy in a world that was and is still struggling to absorb the shock of Darwin's cosmological vision, of modern professional specialization, of fundamental socioeconomic transformation, and of an escalating series of great wars that marked the emergence of the era we now call the age of globalization.[4]

Even Dewey's frequent use of the singular term *metaphysic* in the 1890's and early 1900's suggests a play on the antique word "physic" that still was in use at that time among common people in many parts of America, both as a noun for a traditional medical remedy, including natural herbs and waters, and as a verb for acting to remedy or to heal. In this antique usage, a "physician" is one who uses such remedies and who acts to heal wounds, breakages, and diseases of all kinds in order to restore that great good on which all other goods depend—an active state of mind-body health—along with the habits, tendencies, and means of support to maintain it. In calling for a new "metaphysic," Dewey calls for a paradigm shift: from a world vision in which stability reigns and there is nothing new under the sun, to one in which deeper processes gradually transform even the most stable entities, the mountains and fixed species of our inherited metaphysical map. We need a continuously redrawn map of our world of experience, Dewey urged, one that guides new inquiries for better remedies while acknowledging that, over time, the old diagnostic tools and remedies have lost their "truth" and efficacy to heal, so that even our healers themselves are threatened by mutated new forms of disease, wounds, and breakage within an actual world of human existence that is sometimes stable and sometimes precarious as it affects all we hope for.

If we take seriously Dewey's health metaphor and his reclaimed antique vocabulary, a "meta-physic" is a reflection on and a remedy for the traditional remedies, diagnostic tools, and therapeutic models used by those whose callings, gifts, and professional trainings permit and prepare them to intervene in the course of others' lives in order to promote individual and social health. Its "meta-" quality signals a periodic, reflective stepping back from the daily work of these various "healing" arts and sciences for the purpose of reconsidering their particular problems, practices, and local paradigms from the perspective of a wider experience and a broader set of guiding ideals. If we imagine the full company of these healing professionals as including not only "physicians" in our specialized contemporary sense but all of those who are charged with studying and promoting the diverse prerequisites of health for social individuals and the communities of which they are always and indivisibly members, the work of "metaphysic" is to critique and continuously recreate an inquiry-guiding and imagination-stirring "big picture" or "background map" of the world of humanly experienced and "experieneceable" general traits or conditions of existence—both those that are common to us as humans and those that are common to the wider natural world within which our lives arise and on which they depend.

Remember, Dewey's metaphysics is never a priori. Rather, his "low-rise" metaphysics is always a product of inquiry as Hickman and Haddock Seigfried so aptly describe it later in this book. Nonetheless, once we have the results of those inquiries in many different cultural domains and have made the necessary connections among them, we can use the resulting metaphysics and any other products of inquiry to guide future inquiry, just as Dewey says.

Ideally, this big picture or background map serves to coordinate and guide ongoing processes of criticism and the reconstruction of the specific theories and practices of the diverse "health"-related sciences and arts in light of the overall growth of our experience and knowledge within a world that has shown itself to be stable in many respects over long periods of time, yet always changing, and sometimes bursting forth in startling events that mark the beginning of new eras when the accumulated effects of ongoing change processes have achieved a "critical mass." Such era-inaugurating, experience-reframing events—including 9/11—signal the need for new therapeutic models, new diagnostic tools, and new remedies for healing both chronic and new wounds, breakages, and diseases, and also for instituting various new contributing factors to the "health" of this new era's social individuals and their communities, local and global.

The job of the Deweyan "metaphysician"—one aspect of the work of philosophy as he conceived of it—is to lead or at least to provoke critical updating of the "big picture," to note the new contributions of the various sciences and arts that require its overall adjustment, to serve as a "liaison officer" among them in noting discoveries and new problems in any of them that call for mutual adjustments among all of them, and to encourage and perhaps to participate in new inquiries (disciplinary and interdisciplinary) that will help improve and apply the "big picture" as a therapeutic meta-tool for remedying specific local and global problems of daily living— what Dewey called "the problems of men"—which may, in turn, yield generality-suggesting results for the future updating of the "big picture." That is, the Deweyan metaphysician plays a more or less specialized role within the creation, application, and critical revision of the "big picture" that itself serves *both* as an integrative repository for the most stable and general kinds of fallible, continuously revisable knowledge, *and* as a guiding framework-as-tool for teaching, updating, and applying the various disciplinary and interdisciplinary diagnostic and therapeutic models and practices that seek to restore and promote individual and social health in daily living, including in times of crisis. This is why Dewey called for a "metaphysic of the common man," as R. W. Sleeper has emphasized in arguing that we should retain the term *metaphysics* as well as the Deweyan project of reconstructing the traditional philosophical field of metaphysics as an important element of contemporary pragmatism's engagement with both the academic philosophical community and the wider local, national, and global "publics" we are called as philosophers to serve.[5]

As I understand what Dewey meant by this seemingly ironic or oxymoronic characterization of a new pragmatist metaphysics, the "common man" is both patient and agent-contributor to the various problem-specific projects of healing, and also to the ongoing work of updating the kind of metaphysical "big picture" that can be used to promote the broad ideal of general "health" at the individual, communal, and world levels. Such continuous updating is important, because a reliably current though always dynamic "big picture" is a key tool for producing and coordinating "local ground maps" that can guide, reflect findings, and assist in mid-course readjustments within problem-specific, health-directed projects of inquiry and therapeutic reconstruction. Thus the common person's democratic role within Dewey's "metaphysic" must be double, or even triple: (1) The general and specific problems of the common person, not the problems of philosophers, are its focus as a key element of the kind of philosophy that can heal, restore our hopes, and refit the world for them; (2) The common person must play an important role in inquiry, helping to diagnose as well as to devise and apply context-specific remedies to those local and global problems; (3) The common person may contribute to the ongoing readjustment of the "big picture" that guides such a "metaphysic," including when she or he reflects with others on their shared local and global experience of human living, with its occasional splendors, its episodic shocks, and its ongoing problems and challenges.

Putting Dewey's Democratic Metaphysic to Work
in Democratic Communicative Action

Dewey's famous remedy for the "ailments" of democracy at all
levels and in all contexts was "more democracy"—by which he
meant not more votes, or polls, or elite-run government
bureaus charging to the rescue without consulting affected
citizens about what to do, but rather democratic communicative
actions such as those he described in the 1932 *Ethics* (LW: 7), in
which all participate freely and as equals, contributing and
receiving ideas and values, and in the process, changing minds,
hearts, moods, and motives in ways that allow new, world-
changing institutions and projects of effective collaborative
action to come into existence.[6] In fact, such democratic
communicative action can inaugurate a series of changes so
deep and new creations so profound that it is "a wonder by the
side of which transubstantiation pales," as Dewey wrote in
Experience and Nature, expressing in that passage communicative
action's inexplicably "miraculous" nature when it is interpreted
in terms of a still widely shared, static, physicalist "big map"
that fails to account for this real possibility we actually glimpse
every day, and occasionally see writ large on great days such as
the one on which Martin Luther King Jr. gave his "I Have a
Dream" speech.[7]

Communicative action, as Dewey understood it, is always
context-specific, expressed in local tongues, engaging local
anxieties and hopes, referring to local materials, and with local
body-minds doing the listening, the speaking, the feeling-
thinking, and the heavy lifting. Yet the general traits of
existence and those of human experience that these local
contexts and localized communicative actions reveal and
contribute to the continuous recreation of a Deweyan
metaphysic's "background picture" that can reveal actual or
potential areas of linkage and transference of findings and
remedies to other contexts—provided that this is done with
great care while drawing upon the contribution of local patient-
agents to the diagnostic and therapeutic process—allow us to
learn from one another, to act in solidarity with one another
across wide geographic and cultural distances, and to teach

lessons about past actions as guides to the therapy-planning process Dewey recommended to us in *Human Nature and Conduct* (MW: 14): critically retrieving a "big picture" of past actions, events, and their consequences from memory, factoring in the new in considering its lessons for our present choices, and then engaging in "dramatic rehearsals" of alternative courses of action with their probable consequences to see what choice we can best live with, given the real risks and rewards involved.[8]

Though we do not always need to *call* it "metaphysics," engaging explicitly in what Hickman calls a Deweyan "low-rise" metaphysics often is helpful and occasionally necessary in three important arenas of communicative action in our post-9/11 era: (1) in publicly addressing problems of democratic cultural reinhabitation that have become vitally important in American living and in America's impact on our now-globalized world; (2) in philosophically challenging many of our academic colleagues' continuing preoccupation with "the problems of philosophers" that keeps them from helping out as they could and should with the urgent problems of common living, and occasionally leads them to become practical obstacles to democratic transformation in our culture and our political life; and (3) in our personal reflections and reflective dialogues with our most-trusted others that aim to diagnose what is going on with us and with our world, so that we can creatively imagine therapies that will reconstruct our habits of thinking and acting in ways that will begin to relieve what ails us, and that will prepare us to participate effectively in the other two, wider kinds of therapeutic communicative action.

Some of those who have been patient with me this far may find this claim absurd. They may wonder how any kind of metaphysics, even a Deweyan kind, could have any practical relevance to urgent contemporary problems, and they may worry that focusing attention on tidying up "events," "general traits," "experience," "existence," and other standard bits of furniture in the House of Metaphysics will only mislead us and use up that limited supply of time and energy that is urgently needed now for our context-specific existential and political work. Haddock Seigfried has made such a strong case for this worry that my own advocacy of a Deweyan "metaphysic" must come with a warning label that refers the reader to her reasons for caution.[9] Moreover, she and others may be right when they, with Rorty, call for giving up on at least some of our academic colleagues who are still determined to focus on "the problems of philosophers," arguing that further efforts to reach them are wasted and distract us from more important work we may be able to accomplish if we give it our single-minded best efforts. Finally, for those who, like Rorty and many contemporary thinkers in Germany, find themselves haunted by the metaphysical miscarriages of a still-present past, the suggestion that a metaphysics of any kind may be helpful to our twenty-first century personal reflections and in our therapeutic course-setting dialogues with those whose lives most closely touch our own may seem both absurd and dangerous. Nonetheless, I suggest that employing a Deweyan low rise metaphysics as a background map and therapeutic tool—sometimes explicitly and always implicitly—is necessary, even unavoidable, within all three of these important arenas of communicative action *if* we are to frame and advance the kinds of critical and reconstructive democratic inquiries that will be necessary if we are to achieve an urgently needed, more deeply democratic cultural revitalization and political reinhabitation in America, and in America's relation to the rest of the world. Again, please let me explain.

Many of our problems in American public life today are worsened, and even created in part, by metaphysical mistakes. Some of these metaphysical mistakes are inherited from earlier periods of our nation's and Western civilization's history—they are ways of thinking that many people have found comforting and motivating as "folk remedies" that can counter or cover over a widespread mood of fear and anxiety that has gripped many since 9/11, America's subsequent economic downturn, and our nation's entry into two costly wars of questionable legitimacy and limited effectiveness. Some of these metaphysical mistakes have been specifically prescribed by unwisely trusted, so-called "conservative" political, economic, legal, religious, and cultural leaders, either to advance their other agendas or because they themselves sincerely believe in them. The composite metaphysical "big picture" they now widely employ for these purposes can be evoked by sketching even a few of its elements:

1. Individuals are thought of as atomic in their separateness and as unchangeably given in their personalities and values ("I am what I am").

2. Expansive individual property rights and related life aspirations are thought of as sacred, primitive, part of the "American dream," and as properly safe from criticism ("I gotta be me" and "If I can make it there, I can make it anywhere").

3. Individual political opinions are thought of as emerging in a state of final completeness from the inner sanctum of such a unique, given, property-oriented self, so that they can be collected and aggregated in "objective" public opinion polls that allegedly do not influence public opinion, and then simply "represented" by elected officials who do not reshape or significantly "spin" them.

4. At the same time, the American nation is thought of as a unitary entity with its own overriding "interests" that need not be known about in their particularity in order to be affirmed by each and all of its individual citizen-members.

5. This American nation is thought of as having a unique, privileged place in the world, not only richer and stronger than other nations but wiser, freer, better in every way.

6. The voice of this American nation, speaking to its citizens through leaders elected by a majority of those whose votes are counted—or more accurately, by America's antique aggregative institution, the Electoral College—is thought to trump the voices of its individual citizen-members, whose views and values simply are judged by it to be intellectually and morally wrong if not in agreement with it, and whose

aspirations and conduct are expected to be
brought into patriotic conformity with it after
such errors are pointed out.[10]

7. Other nations and individuals are thought of as to
be converted, rescued, or forced to agree in their
conduct with this vision of America as the leading
nation of history's advance in the twenty-first
century ("God is on our side").

When it is sketched explicitly, even to this limited extent,
the currently dominant, so-called "conservative" American
"big picture" displays some major flaws that do and must keep
it from guiding true, effective, and sustainable remedies for
what ails us now. First, it is hopelessly inconsistent—the first
three elements flatly contradict the last four, so that this "big
picture" cannot be rescued, either by the kind of "two-levels
systems analysis" that is popular now among many social
theorists, including Habermas, or by the sincere efforts of
many American citizens to really believe, feel, and live out in
practice all that it requires of them. Second, it is profoundly
undemocratic in ways that go to opposite extremes: Whereas
the first three elements aim toward a libertarian (neoconservative and neoliberal) individualism that has no room for
the kinds of productive dialogues, give-and-take, practical
sharing, and committed common effort that deep democracy
requires, the last four elements aim toward a national totality
that treats individual claims of justice and freedom as
superficial, thus undermining our nation's costly achievements
of civil rights and liberties, of real respect for the dissenting
opinion of the loyal opposition, and of recognition of the
great mistakes in our nation's past that should lead us all to say
"never again."

However, instead of revealing and rejecting these profound
errors in our nation's currently dominant "big picture," most
American opponents of the disastrous errors of commission and
omission in our nation's post-9/11 public policies simply try to
tweak it or critique its applications, while having nothing
fundamentally different to propose as a metaphysical counter-

vision or as a cultural and political therapeutic. This shows the error in Rawls's thinking, that an overlapping democratic consensus that is "political, not metaphysical" would be enough to guide the American polity or any other democratic nation-state in the twenty-first century We may not need complete agreement all the way down and in every element of our group-linked "big pictures," but we clearly cannot avoid taking these background pictures into account; and when profound errors and inconsistencies in them emerge and make a major difference in public matters, we must make these background "big pictures" themselves public matters, and we must attempt to critically clarify and to collaboratively remedy them as needed.

Who can and should try to remedy these profoundly dangerous mistakes in America's currently dominant metaphysical "big picture," and how can it best be done? Given our long-term American cultural tendency to turn to religion in times of trouble, we might think that the best spokespersons for a team of metaphysical healing specialists from various fields and disciplines would be religious leaders, especially if we could find some with Martin Luther King Jr.'s critical philosophical training, diagnostic skills, creative visioning gift, collaborative model of inquiry, and personal habits of courage and hope. There are *some* religious leaders of this kind among us now, and the fact that they are *not yet* acknowledged as national leaders and world figures should not delay our support for their efforts. For many reasons, however, we cannot rely on them alone or on the religious domain of our national culture exclusively as the focus of much-needed projects of metaphysical reconstruction within our shared national culture.

Who else needs to critique and offer counterproposals to the currently dominant metaphysical "big pictures" that dominate American public discourse and block our path to shared healing and democratic social hope? I have space here only to suggest some key members of a deeply democratic metaphysical therapy team that may be able to remedy America's now-epidemic disease if they work together after undergoing a refresher course in Dewey's metaphysic:

- Politicians—local, regional, national, international
- Intellectual leaders, including philosophers and other social critics and theorists
- Natural scientists, including physicists, biologists, and human physiologists
- Health care practitioners and frontline social service providers
- Artists of all kinds—filmmakers and actors, television producers and writers, composers and musicians, dancers, painters and illustrators, storytellers, novelists and poets, including spoken word poets, and roots hip-hop artists of all the other genres
- News media professionals and bloggers
- Educators at all levels and in all kinds of institutions
- Opinion leaders who are valued for their wisdom
- Ordinary citizens, using their democratic communicative powers in the face-to-face transactions of daily living and reflection with friends, in e-mails and letters to one another and to all of the other aforementioned kinds of social actors, in public protests large and small, and in their choices in the marketplace and other arenas of future making

Working in their own ways, such diverse "metaphysical" healers can initiate the new American process of community building that Campbell calls for, creating conditions for the kinds of dialogue amidst our differences Garrison calls for, and tempering this process with the tools of contemporary "border-crossing" research that Neubert rightly points out are already available to us.

Notes

1. I am grateful to Seth Joshua Thomas for helping me see "health" as a key philosophical focus and an extended metaphor in Dewey's work. Thomas's framing of this topic has illuminated this deep pattern in Dewey's work for me, helping me to express my sense of how to understand and treat the post-9/11 American "democratic disease." I am grateful to Reich and Neubert, as well as to Hickman,

for the invitation to present an earlier version of this chapter at the Inaugural Conference of the Köln Dewey Center, and to all of the participants in that conference for a lively discussion. Finally, I am grateful to participants in the New York Pragmatist Forum for taking this version of the chapter under their advisement.

2. "Established democracies" is one of Robert Dahl's (1998) terms within his insightful analysis of democracy's international scope and prospects for progress in the twenty-first century in his *On Democracy*. For my earlier discussion of the fourfold "democratic disease" that I believe now plagues America, see my *Deep Democracy: Community, Diversity, and Transformation* (1999, 2ff iv).

3. Here Rorty quotes from Dewey's "Maeterlinck's Philosophy of Life" (MW 6, 1978: 135). For Rawls's argument that we can do political philosophy without metaphysics, including adequately addressing moral issues of justice, see his 1985 essay, "Political not Metaphysical," his 1995 "Reply to Habermas," and his fuller development of these ideas in *Political Liberalism* (New York: Columbia University Press, 1996).

4. See the essay by Dewey's student, John Herman Randall Jr. (1939, 93).

5. See R. W. Sleeper's magisterial work, *The Necessity of Pragmatism: John Dewey's Conception of Philosophy* (New Haven, CT: Yale University Press, 1986).

6. See LW 7: 348–49.

7. LW 1: 132.

8. See Dewey's MW 14: 132.

9. See Haddock Seigfried (2004, 53–78). For contrasting views by other Deweyan pragmatists who see a continuing need for some kind of metaphysic(s), though they may disagree with one another about how to characterize and advance it, see work by Thomas Alexander, R. W. Sleeper, Jim Garrison, Raymond Boisvert, and William Myers. I am grateful to Barbara Lowe for her careful and insightful treatment of this controversy in the footnotes of her doctoral dissertation, *Beyond recognition: A feminist-pragmatist account of moral agency* (New York: Fordham University Press, 2005).

10. Dewey was already critical of the anti-democratic purpose and tendencies of the Electoral College in *The Public and Its Problems*

(LW 2). Since the 2000 elections, in which it combined with a 5–4 Supreme Court decision to award the American presidency to George W. Bush, even though Albert H. Gore clearly won the popular vote. With all of the division, dishonesty, and disheartening decisions that have flowed from that outcome, it is now clear that the impact of this antique institution is an obstacle to reclaiming and deepening American democracy that can no longer be tolerated.

Works Cited

Dahl, R. 1998. *On democracy*. New Haven: Yale University Press.

Green, J. 1999. *Deep democracy: Community, diversity, and transformation*. New York: Rowman & Littlefield.

Lowe, B. 2005. *Beyond recognition: A feminist-pragmatist account of moral agency*. New York: Fordham University Press.

Randall, J. R., Jr. 1939. Dewey's interpretation of the history of philosophy. In *The philosophy of John Dewey*, ed. Paul Authur Schiepp and Lewis Edwin Hahn. LaSalle, IL: Open Court, 75–102 vol. 1.

Rawls, J. 1985. Political not Metaphysical. *Philosophy and Public Affairs* 14: 223–52.

———. 1995. Reply to Habermas. *The Journal of Philosophy* 92:3: 132–80.

———. 1996. *Political liberalism*. New York: Columbia University Press.

Rorty, R. 1998: *Achieving our country: Leftist thought in twentieth-century America*. Cambridge, MA, and London: Harvard University Press.

———. 1999). *Philosophy and Social Hope*. New York: Penguin.

Seigfried, C. H. 2004. Ghosts walking underground: Dewey's vanishing metaphysics," *Transactions of the Charles S. Peirce Society* XL:1 (Winter): 53–78.

Sleeper, R. W. 1986. *The necessity of pragmatism: John Dewey's conception of philosophy*. New Haven, CT: Yale University Press.

Chapter 3

Democracy and Education after Dewey—Pragmatist Implications for Constructivist Pedagogy

Kersten Reich

In 1916, John Dewey published his work *Democracy and Education* (MW 9), which subsequently became a pedagogic-philosophical classic and was translated into German in 1930. Unfortunately, the German version used misleading translations of some of Dewey's central terms, particularly as the translator was often unable to comprehend adequately the meaning as well as the philosophical context of Dewey's pragmatism.[1]

However, in 1930 it is unlikely that *any* translation could have helped carry Dewey's democratic spirit to Germany. His ideas of democracy as a way of life based on the far-reaching participation of all citizens in democratic processes were contrary to the dominant political tendencies in Germany. This incompatibility is evident in the face of the fatal historic developments in the early 1930s. In Germany, the dominance of anti-democratic forces led to the victory of National Socialism. After the downfall of Hitler's regime in 1945, German education largely fell back on the traditional model of a strongly selective educational system.

The term *community* (*Gemeinschaft*) was particularly problematic. Dewey's idea of it presupposed the plurality of a social group, allowing dissimilarities within. In contrast, the German debate about *Gemeinschaft* often was characterized by notions of uniformity and subordination, especially after the experience of the Nazi *Volksgemeinschaft*.

In all international school systems community is regarded as one of the essential features of a comprehensive school, in which pupils are jointly educated until around age sixteen. In Germany, however, there has been a countermovement to this general trend in reaction to National Socialism. The traditional model of a tripartite secondary school system beginning at age ten has always been focused, ideally, on the expectation of the worth of individual learning, thus neglecting interaction and cooperation of learners. Due to this, the German school system today not only ranks low in international school performance tests but also occupies an isolated position with its early selection process that falls short of its confessed expectations (cf. Schnepf 2002). And what is even worse, in reaction to this situation it is increasingly developing into a multidivisional system in which special schools for so-called "learners with learning disabilities" are playing a growing role.

Generally, these tendencies show an unfortunate relationship between democracy and education in Germany. After 1945, the so-called German school reform did not adequately notice and develop the democratization of education according to Dewey or other democratic school reforms. We still carry the burden of these structural problems today, as our outdated school system turns out to be increasingly anti-democratic in its institutional setting.

I trace this idea by taking up Dewey's argumentation of 1916 with regard to the relationship of democracy and education (section 1). Then I discuss some of the pragmatist implications of democracy and education for a constructivist approach (section 2). At the end of this chapter I briefly and critically reflect on the anti-democratic tendencies of the German school system using Dewey's criteria (section 3).

1. Democracy and Education according to Dewey

In the following I give a short introduction to Dewey's approach. I concentrate mainly on "democracy and education," especially the chapter "The Democratic Conception in Education" (MW 9: 87 ff.). One of Dewey's main assumptions in this chapter is that the social organization of groups also requires their education from within. "Since education is a social process, and there are many kinds of societies, a criterion for educational criticism and construction implies a *particular* social ideal" (105). A democratic society is only one of many possible social constructions. It is characterized not only by traditions and a necessary transmission of customs and habits but also by the fact that it allows and promotes developments and social progress within its system.[2] The term *growth*, which Dewey uses to describe a democratic concept of education (cf. e.g., 46 ff.), aims at developing flexible habits that act in the world in accordance with its resources.[3] Habits are active forces of adaptation within an environment in the sense of accommodation and assimilation. "Growth," in terms of a democratic education, means, for instance, the intentional and deliberate use of impulses and forces for forward development, and this in particular implies avoidance of mere imitation, routines, and reproductions. It also attempts to initiate an intentional social change that will enable the participation of all.

Against this background, there are two essential criteria for Dewey in describing a democratic community (89 ff.):

1. Dewey points out that in any social group "we find some interest in common" (89). But if we look for democracy, we have to ask an important question: How numerous and varied are the consciously shared interests within a community? Democratic growth presupposes the existence of diverse interests. Dewey says: "Diversity of stimulation means novelty, and novelty means challenge to thought" (90). Diversity cannot develop when there are "rigid class lines preventing ade-

quate interplay of experiences" (90). Democracy needs "reciprocity of interest" (91). Its prosperity rests on recognition and understanding of different interests within the framework of social control. Using modern terminology, we can say that plurality of interests shared within a community is a necessary precondition of education for democracy.

2. Dewey argues that in any social group "we find a certain amount of interaction and cooperative intercourse with other groups" (89). Again, this involves an important question for democratic development: How complete and unhindered is the exchange taking place with other communities? Democracy can grow (in families as in nations) more efficiently if interaction takes place not only between social groups of one common interest, one nation, or one special society but when people continually create, and constantly readjust, new challenges within the frame of social change by different interactions with different interpretive communities, families, nations, or societies.

Dewey argues that both principles are of crucial importance for education (93). Democratic societies following these principles always show a general interest in liberal and systematic education. Contrary to an education and instruction of compliant subjects or any authoritarian subordination, the development of a democratic education must be the expression of a free and deliberate selection of consciously shared interests. Here democratic life can develop through common relations and mutual communication, which again will extend the range of possibility for independent action for individuals who interact with each other in their own interests, as well as those of others. It is necessary for every participant to communicate his or her own interests to others. Based on this approach, we are able to begin to overcome racism, class separation, and nationalism. According to Dewey, these are three conditions that keep human beings from attaining greater self-development.

If his two democratic criteria are followed and realized in everyday life and in education, then a larger diversity of interests may be established. This diversity gives people the chance to come into contact with one another, so that they may discover personal potentials as well as new opportunities for interaction. The more group interests are allowed to develop in varying ways, and the less they follow group egoisms or partial interests, the better an individual's chances seem to be in a democracy. This is what eventually enables democratic life. At the same time, it broadens the basis of opportunities for an education that, in its democratic orientation, always needs to develop a diversity and dissimilarity of prospects against the background of mutual respect. This can be realized by enabling the growth of the individual abilities of all members of a society in a sustained and socially balanced way, thus aiding the continual expansion of the width and diversity of interests.

Dewey offers two examples of a possible application of both criteria. As a negative example he mentions criminal gangs (89). Within such gangs—which may, for instance, remind us of the Mafia—relationships are very tight, and the common basis of interests is defined very narrowly.

If we apply the first criterion, we critically observe a tendency toward a strong partiality. In consequence, the group members are neither offered new, different interests nor a continuous growth of opportunities. By being fixated on money and a "common interest in plunder," all perspectives are narrowed.

The second criterion may be applied as follows: Although it is a social group, the free intercourse with other groups is systematically impeded, and harsh punishment threatens to follow any violation of this rule. As a generalized consequence, Dewey concludes, "An undesirable society... is one which internally and externally sets up barriers to free intercourse and communication of experience" (105). As a positive example, Dewey mentions the family:

> If we take, on the other hand, the kind of family life which illustrates the standard, we find that there are material, intellectual, aesthetic interests in which all participate and that the progress of one member has worth for the experience of other members—it

is readily communicable—and that the family is not an isolated whole, but enters intimately into relationships with business groups, with schools, with all the agencies of culture, as well as with other similar groups, and that it plays a due part in the political organization and in return receives support from it. (89)

The ideal of the American nuclear family cannot be more distinctly marked than by contrasting it to the Mafia or any other gang or anti-democratic group. Yet this idealization is, from today's perspective, as well as with regard to Dewey's complete works, certainly too coarse in its simplification.[4] This becomes especially clear if we, using the same metaphor, consider the Mafia a "big family." The term *family*, on its own, cannot be regarded as sufficient in order to describe the ideal as imagined by Dewey. This example alone is not sufficient to substantiate the given principles. To do so, Dewey would need to apply the principles individually in each and every case to show their critical, practical relevance in a pragmatist way. And he would need to take into account what he himself discussed in the beginning of this chapter, that is, the question of whether something happens by emerging from norms and ideals de jure, or whether it is actually and—in being executed—realistically achieved de facto in practice. The criteria can only sufficiently be substantiated if ideal conditions are not only contrasted in an abstract way, but concrete cases are inquired into de facto. Such evidence should at least be critically examined with regard to its prerequisites and conditions. It would then become apparent that the idealized standard family is somehow problematic. This is due to the fact that Dewey uses it as an illustrative example, yet at the same time he seems to succumb to the idealization itself.

According to Dewey's notion of a good community, both criteria have to be taken into account. They form a basis for further conclusions (cf. also Campbell 1998, 23 ff.).[5] Interaction is an essential prerequisite here. Because human beings need to interact with each other, they also need to synchronize their actions. This is regarded as a condition for action to take place within a community, but it also shows why human beings are in need of a community, as they are unable to survive on their own and without any interaction. Synchronizations of actions in interactions enable the formation of shared interests and joint actions. Cooperation is—in a very different way—a basic prerequisite for a good community. Such common interests are secured by the shared values provided by education. However, the community of values must avoid a standstill. This is why, according to Dewey, it would be fatal if the community of education were narrowed to the special interests of specific groups. Dewey claims that the "good" can only be found and time and again has to be rediscovered by comprehensive application of the two criteria. Therefore, the two basic criteria should be constantly present in our communications. They need to be rooted as common values in our common experiences in order to secure and develop democracy in the long run. The growth of differences is the basis of democratic change and development. At the same time, the criteria themselves form a necessary democratic commonality. The purposeful interest in this commonality must be realized as a plurality of interests that has to reject the intention to subordinate all interests to one or a few dominant perspectives.

Starting from this basis, education needs to take part in the task of realizing the implementation of diversity and democratic commonalities. This includes the ability of all group members to make deliberate decisions about their sense of shared values. Education can only succeed in this task if it is experienced as a democracy on a small scale.[6] Basically, even the youngest members of a society or community need to have freedom of choice in order to secure the application of the two criteria. Following Dewey's approach, education is therefore confronted with a paradoxical task. It must increase the diversity of human interests and abilities, the plurality, multiculturalism, and other aspects of growth in society. At the same time, it must develop a common understanding of the necessity of a general recognition of this diversity as a central value of democracy. This paradox of the relation between diversity and commonality is but another manifestation of the fundamental democratic paradox between freedom and solidarity (cf. Mouffe 1994, 1996).

2. A Constructivist Interpretation of Dewey's Criteria

By building on these two criteria, Dewey has developed general categories of observation that help judge and evaluate social groups in their interactions. As observers we seem to be free in our observations, yet this freedom is always tied to a specific form of participation. Our participation in applying Dewey's democratic theory is based on the condition that we regard his criteria as meaningful. Therefore, I would like to ask how convincing these criteria are from a constructivist perspective. In this context the following aspects especially attracted my attention.

2.1. The Role of the Criteria in Dewey's Text

The choice of Dewey's criteria appears at first sight to be rather random and also surprising, even in the context of the argumentation in *Democracy and Education*. In the preceding chapters, Dewey has indeed elaborated on the necessity of education within a framework of renewal of life and cultural development. He has characterized education primarily as a social function and also has related it to the needs of a social community. Further, he has particularly emphasized the importance of growth and criticized the reduction of education to a mere reflection of established forms of life or only disciplinary actions to preserve culture. He also has distinguished education as conservative and progressive with its political implications and has, in particular, critically argued against the consequences of the mere reproduction of current habits, against the overemphasis on genetics, and against the fact that so many pedagogical approaches orientate themselves toward the past. Nevertheless, he has failed to develop a systematic theory of social systems or groups that may help understand why exactly these two criteria, as postulated by him, should, respectively, have to be given priority in serving as general criteria. Although it is clear that Dewey makes conclusions about the state of democracy and education within social groups from the way they interact, still, the criteria as well as the examples seem to appear in the text without any further preparation. They are normatively set and structure the text without having undergone any explicit introduction.

On the other hand, and at second view, we can realize that there is an implicit argumentation about them in Dewey's text. After introducing and illustrating the criteria, Dewey goes on to devote his attention in three larger steps to the history of education with regard to its implications for democracy. In this discussion it turns out that his criteria are not at all as arbitrary as one might have guessed at first sight. Although it requires a close reading between the lines, the historic interpretation does contain, in my opinion, three essential arguments:

1. The example of the criminal gang shows in a negative way what will happen if social groups merely pay attention to their own interests, excluding and fighting against all other groups. This attitude can be substantiated in many historic situations and appears to be absolutely typical for all anti- or predemocratic structures. Dewey implicitly substantiates both criteria by picking out specific situations in order to illustrate his theses. Plato's approach is named as a highly relevant educational philosophy in this context. According to Dewey, Plato's theory contains many positive educational basics, but he criticizes the fact that Plato offers no approach that seizes the endless plurality of human activity. This plurality is neglected both according to its individual and its social group aspects (cf. MW 9: 94). His criticism does not solely aim to situate Plato within the context of antiquity. Instead, Dewey inquires into the meaning of this theory in his own time and in relation to the challenges of modernity. The essential factors that are rigidly limiting the individuals' different developmental prospects according to their affinities and abilities are, for example, the strict segmentation into classes, the lack of consideration for the uniqueness of individuals, the social division by supposedly natural determination, and the negation of dynamic change within societies.

This is contrary to a democratic approach that
appreciates the uniqueness of individuals and claims
recognition of difference as a prerequisite for
advancing perspectives of acting in a modern society. But Dewey does not naïvely fail to realize that
social change toward modernity is not so much a
product of enlightened reasoning. Rather, it is a
result of changes in modes of production and ways
of life. These changes he regards as being continually tied to constructions of reality that human
beings have ideally created for their orientation
through forms of production and trade, traffic and
travel, migration and media, or science in its manifold forms. These ideas have been materialized in
culture and thus realized as prerequisites for further
perspectives of acting and thinking. The standard of
living that was reached at the beginning of the
twentieth-century represents for Dewey the hope
that his two criteria of democratization can be realized to a much larger extent than in the past. This
possibility depends on the agreement of humans
about a necessary democratization based on the
claimed standards of diversity within their interests.
And they would have to do this in an intentional,
socially lived manner. Education as a process plays
the leading part in such a democratization. Because
social groups construct their own norms and constantly need to readjust to changing interests
throughout history, this process will always remain
incomplete. When critically evaluating this process,
both criteria turn out to be very helpful as a means
to observe, to participate, and to act in democracy.

2. Dewey regards the individualistic ideals and naturalistic ideas of eighteenth-century education in the
context of a social battle in which the child's or subject's nature was constructed specifically to fight the
feudal system. But his analyses, for example, on
Rousseau's naturalism, are somewhat brief. Dewey
misses the fact that Rousseau himself had already

realized that the natural conditions and their driving forces (*amour de soi, amour propre*) have to be regarded as logical hypotheses rather than as direct copies of a historic reality. Seen from a constructivist perspective, Rousseau, by a deliberate move, projected the social assumptions of his age into nature to make them socially plausible. This also applies to Dewey himself. His two criteria display a clear relation to the social interests of progressive liberal groups in the American society of 1916, although he often neglects to expose his position as a generalization of specific interests in a specific historical context.

Further, Rousseau, in his *The Social Contract* ([1761] 1988), provided essential preparatory work for the foundations of a democratic education in Dewey's sense, which, oddly enough, Dewey does not mention at all in this passage. Although he does not elaborate on the differences between *Emile* ([1762] 1979) and *The Social Contract*, he nevertheless knows of them. This becomes apparent in his brief mention of the fact that in the context of nonfeudal social relations, Rousseau regards the perspective of the free citizen as being superior to the rather individualistic perspective of *Emile*. According to Rousseau, before a democratic revolution can fulfill its expectations, every individual needs to become a free citizen. And natural education, for him, is the means for effecting this change.

This is where Dewey clearly criticizes and goes beyond Rousseau's argumentation. At the beginning of the twentieth-century, he can take his start from the historical success of civil society as a condition for education. What Dewey criticizes from this perspective is the overestimation of individualism and naturalistic idealizations that have not withstood social reality. The gap between ideals and social reality—particularly

with Johann Pestalozzi—showed him the important steps that still had to be taken in the process
of establishing a public school system, quite apart
from the fact that this system had to be democratically formed by democratic revolutions, which
formed the political context that directly confronted Dewey in 1916. Within this process,
Dewey places emphasis on a social rather than a
national orientation, because to him only a
transnational orientation will help develop a comprehensive democracy for all human beings. He
showed a keen sense for the potential catastro-
phes, which did indeed come true during the first
half of the twentieth-century in countries where
nationalism assumed a dominant position in education and social development. Dewey is
extremely careful in his historic interpretations,
since he believes social conceptions lose their significance in education if they are not reconstructed in a historical and critical way within
their changing contexts (MW 9: 102).
Nevertheless, the example of nationalism serves
him well in illustrating and clarifying the relevance of his second criterion. Only a discourse
crossing national and other borders can ensure
that modern societies succeed in democratically
organizing social change. Such discourse presupposes a pluralistic universe of interpretive communities. Based on these arguments drawn from his
democratic criteria, Dewey thinks that any confusion of social aims with national or similar narrowly oriented ones implies a threat to democracy.
3. Although the development of society in 1916
   already shows a comprehensive market-related
   exchange, and although capitalism in its manifold
   shapes tends to assume a globalized form—
   Dewey talks of "interdependencies and cooperation among the peoples inhabiting different
   countries" (103)—still the individual nations

maintain a strong self-interest and strive for exclusion in order to secure their own sovereignty. At the same time, there is the development of a comprehensive and pluralistic ethnic community, which Dewey supported effectively and which, already in 1916, he clearly formulates as fundamental for the design of education: "Is it possible for an educational system to be conducted by a national state and yet the full social ends of the educative process not be restricted, constrained, and corrupted?" (104).

From this historic perspective, interests in national societies were primarily centered around the question of class. Dewey described severe social inequalities in the societies of his time, which degraded many people to being mere tools of a minority. The society's dominant view of the outside world was very much determined by questions of patriotism and values regarding mankind and humanity on the whole. National prejudices could be relativized and criticized only from a humane perspective within the spectrum of all cultures. What can be done in order to find positive solutions for the problem of enhancing equal chances for the underprivileged as well as advancing human rights in the face of national hegemonies? This is where education meets a crucial social function in assisting the attempts to change the conditions and the environment, to improve prospects and compensate discriminations, and to create greater social justice. It also may provide an understanding of the other as a human being and as part of human development as a whole, instead of regarding the strange as abnormal.

Proceeding from these three exemplary analyses, it becomes evident that the choice of the two criteria is not as arbitrary as it may have seemed initially. Although the reader may not find it easy to detect the connections made by Dewey, we still find that he constructed the two criteria as a political reflected solution in the context of the severe social struggles of his time and that the arguments he found still remain important for our time.

2.2. Dewey's Criteria as Democratic Metaperspectives

As a further possible objection, one could say that both criteria are very general and open to very different interpretations. Particularly, Dewey's example of an ideal family may suggest that he did not sufficiently consider the complexities of social groups.

On the other hand, one could counter that Dewey nevertheless has the basic difficulties of democracy in mind—to enable growth and an extension of options and action prospects in the sense of the growth of individuality, while at the same time being able to imagine and realize basic commonalities through democratic deliberation, to achieve diversity and solidarity within a "good" social group, while at the same time enabling a comprehensive and empathetic exchange with other groups in a diverse society.[7]

Wherever concrete analyses are to be made, both criteria can help recognize and render problematic the limits and difficulties of a community. As Dewey consequently relates this to education, this also shows the minimum requirements of an education, which, in being consciously coeducative, does not lead to a standardized universality but rather enables and encourages differences and individualities in cooperation with others. After all, particularly nowadays, this is the central concern of intercultural and multicultural education theories.

Additionally, such education has to be perceived as democracy on a small scale. In many of his works, Dewey emphasizes that a representative democracy will undermine its own democratic processes if all members of society are not enabled from childhood to carry and develop the meaning and profits of a direct participation in socially determinative decisions. According to him, this is the basis of a lived democracy. In this case we would need communities based on democratic practice from early childhood on.

However, from a constructivist perspective today, we can, to my mind, suggest two important omissions in Dewey's discussions of both criteria.[8]

> 1. With regard to the first criterion, it still applies to our versions of reality constructions today that

growth of differences adds to a broader range of action perspectives and plural chances of interacting. But the democratic development of differences as we have observed in the twentieth-century has by no means resolved the social contradictions of capitalist societies to the extent that Dewey in 1916 hoped for. And, of course, in Dewey's work a lot of differences are missing. Judith Green (1999) points to power-structured relational differences such as culture, class, race, and gender, where Dewey failed to develop a sufficient approach.[9] In addition, our postmodern situation today is characterized by a growing awareness not only of diversity but also of ambivalence in society, a position vividly made clear, for example, by Zygmunt Bauman.[10] Ambivalence in this view means, among other things, that we perceive more soberly that all progress—even of the material kind—has two sides. It often enables a higher standard of living, but it also entails risks of life. The idea of a *risk society*—as advanced, for example, by Ulrich Beck or Anthony Giddens—articulates a view of changes in society that cannot be classified unambiguously as either entirely positive or entirely negative. In our intentionally divided or unintentionally lived wishes and options, values have become more ambiguous, more contradictory, and very often ambivalent. The social separation and divisions in society must be seen in light of this ambivalence. Wealth and standards of living, educational chances, and prospects of ways of life develop very differently for different individuals in the global context. Nowadays, given this individual and global ambiguity of growth, it becomes more and more important to establish new criteria for the limitation of the ecstasies of freedom (in the sense of growing egoism), as well as for advancing solidarity with the less privileged.

2. Regarding Dewey's second criterion, we also must observe today that the development of the last century has not seen a clear breakthrough of his democratic hopes with regard to free intercourse and exchange of social groups across national or other borders. Although to a certain extent institutional forms such as the United Nations have succeeded in securing recognition of diversity on an international scale, there are still a lot of violent conflicts in the world. The problem of enabling consensus and dissent without violence is still an unsolved one. Seen from today's perspective, Dewey in his time still underestimated the question of power as it was later discussed (e.g., by Foucault). The discussion of cultural hegemonies, and the relation of discourses and powers, is a clear step beyond Dewey's political view.

The two marked omissions point to the need for a critical reconstruction of new criteria for democratic development.[11] In what follows I show two lines of possible reconstruction after giving a brief summary of what I have so far discussed.

Both criteria suggested by Dewey in *Democracy and Education* are very valuable metaperspectives as to the norms of practical philosophy and education. To my mind they will continue to be applicable for critical thinking about democracy in our own time. They are not and do not pretend to be a philosophy of the "last word" (Thomas Nagel) for which some other philosophers even today are still searching.[12] Instead, they are pragmatic suggestions, hypotheses finding their only legitimacy in the reconstruction of experiences in changing social contexts or in their application to changing social contexts. Their plausibility or viability has to be acknowledged time and again by interpretive communities within a diverse society on the basis of data and observation, in inquiries and experiments.

Constructivism, as I see it, should follow the line of these pragmatic criteria. Supposing that the first criterion is the minimum basis for the construction of democracy and education, it induces us to ask as a standard for democracy to what extent openness, difference, and growth of extended perspectives of acting can be experienced by all individuals without unjust exclusions and disadvantages. The second criterion as a minimum requirement for democracy refers to mutual recognition of difference and the necessity of cross-border dialogues. It implies a critical discourse on the possibilities and limits of cross-cultural understanding.[13] Although both criteria have to be reconstructed in the application to changing and new contexts, they remain adequate standard tools as a metaperspective open to extensions.

2.3. Two Possible Lines of Reconstruction

In the age of globalization, where democratic practice is undergoing great change, we might find several possible lines of reconstructing Dewey's criteria. In what follows I especially focus on two possible issues.

2.3.1. Observer, Participant, and Agent as Relevant Perspectives.
Dewey conceives his two criteria mainly from a participant perspective. This means that he views democratic processes as equally comprehending all those who participate in them, if only people are ready to realize such a participation for themselves. Applying our theoretical constructs from the participant perspective, however, often makes us prone to erect our own democratic ideals into universally applicable truths, because as participants we easily tend to become neglectful about the limits of our own cultural contexts of participation.

In all this Dewey is aware of the fact that these assumptions and expectations need to be relativized in some way. I quote some passages from *The Public and Its Problems* that further the arguments from *Democracy and Education* and that can illustrate this very well. For instance, with regard to the role of the state, Dewey says: "In concrete fact, in actual and concrete organization and structure, there is no form of state which can be said to be the best: not at least till history is ended, and one can survey all its varied forms" (LW 2: 256).

In this context Dewey does not expect to arrive at any universally applicable theoretical solution. Rather, he continues to refer his criteria for democracy to *inquiry* and the solution of practical problems. In doing so he aims to ensure that one is dealing with real actions rather than mere fictions: "What is needed to direct and make fruitful social inquiry is a method which proceeds on the basis of the interrelations of observable acts and their results" (258). Furthermore, he sees "face-to-face communication" as a vital basis for all social matters: "There is no substitute for the vitality and depth of close and direct intercourse and attachment" (368).

Human happiness and growth require a community, according to the first criterion, but this also means to avoid fixation of definitions as to the nature and character of that community:

> That happiness which is full of content and peace is found only in enduring ties with others, which reach to such depths that they go below the surface of conscious experience to form its undisturbed foundation. No one knows how much of the frothy excitement of life, of mania for motion, of fretful discontent, of need for artificial stimulation, is the expression of frantic search for something to fill the void caused by the loosening of the bonds which hold persons together in immediate community of experience. (369 ff.)

Although it would be hard to refute any of these statements, Dewey also stresses the role of the participant in performing generalizations, which can, from a constructivist perspective, be seen as problematic. For example, one problematic generalization, to my mind, that often appears in Dewey's discourse on science and scientific methods concerns the status of facts both as given and constructed. Although Dewey, in his theory of inquiry, generally acknowledges the cultural construction of facts, there are other places in his works, such as the following quotation from *The Public and Its Problems*, where he seems to regard some facts as simply given: "The more sincerely we appeal to facts, the greater is the importance of the distinction between facts which condition human activity and facts which are conditioned by human activity. In the degree which we ignore this difference, social science becomes pseudo-science" (240).

At this point what is missing is an observer theory, which would have to clarify to what extent facts are always constructs within cultural contexts by observers. Interactive constructivism emphasizes that these observers appear as participants when we ask for the preconditions of their observations, and that they appear as agents when we ask for the actions they make. As a participant in a democracy, for example, we need first of all to decide what structural possibilities we need in order to live democratically—such as through regulations of the state—and furthermore what we can contribute to such a way of living ourselves. At the same time, though, we need to be critical observers of such participation. We need to continually question who sets the criteria that seemingly determine our actions and observations. We need to expand our horizon of observation so as not to succumb to the illusion that certain facts of our time and place are simply given as outer and independent determinations of our own human activities. We must recognize how in action and interaction such facts have been constructed by humans. We also need to ask ourselves, in the processes of constructing our own reality, to what extent we also contribute to "facts" seemingly coming from outside while we are actually involved in the process of creating them.

This self-critical view, which constructivism provides, does not deny the meaning of facts. Rather, we view facts as being connected to the constructions of reality that people create and have created in the past, out of their own interests and needs. In doing so, we do not need to deny that the viability (the practical effectiveness) of such facts can and should be studied and checked through inquiry, especially with regard to existential decisions. Historically, we know that what once seemed to be facts in the sense of the "given" turned out to be temporarily valid constructions replaced by later developments.

Especially focusing on the problem of experts, I discuss this problem in a comparison between Dewey and Bourdieu. In my mind this can show how important it is to see the differences between the roles of observer, participant, and agent. When we consider the role of the public intellectual, it seems necessary to me to exceed a narrow participant perspective.

In an important passage, also from *The Public and Its Problems*, Dewey comments with regard to controversies around the development of the public:

> The essential need, in other words, is the improvement of the methods and conditions of debate, discussion and persuasion. That is the problem of the public. We have asserted that this improvement depends essentially upon freeing and perfecting the processes of inquiry and of dissemination of their conclusions. Inquiry, indeed, is a work which devolves upon experts. But their expertness is not shown in framing and executing policies, but in discovering and making known the facts upon which the former depend. They are technical experts in the sense that scientific investigators and artists manifest expertise. It is not necessary that the many should have the knowledge and skill to carry on the needed investigations; what is required is that they have the ability to judge of the bearing of the knowledge supplied by others upon common concerns. (365)

Dewey has no isolated class of experts in mind: "A class of experts is inevitably so removed from common interests as to become a class with private interests and private knowledge, which in social matters is not knowledge at all" (364). Therefore, the role of experts has to be limited: "No government by experts in which the masses do not have the chance to inform the experts as to their needs can be anything but an oligarchy managed in the interests of the few" (365).[14] Campbell is quite correct (in his chapter in this book) when he observes that those such as Walter Lippmann who thought political concerns exclusively "expert matters" are, in truth, "anti-democrats."

Pierre Bourdieu has intensively researched such "methods and conditions of debate, discussion, and persuasion" in his works, with a special focus on the role of the expert. In short, he is not only far less optimistic than Dewey, but he can actually see no chances for a practical realization of a liberal approach such as Dewey's, which hopes for the good in humans. Bourdieu would respond to Dewey that his approach omits too many conditional factors of participating in modern democracy. In

Bourdieu's theory, these are the well-known concepts such as "habitus, field, and capital."

A *habitus* is "a set of *dispositions* which incline agents to act and react in certain ways," and this could be relatively homogeneous for individuals from a community with a similar background. These dispositions show in a field that is defined as "a structured space of positions in which the positions and their interrelations are determined by the distribution of the different kinds of resources or 'capital' " (Thompson 1991, 14).

Compared to Dewey, who with his concept of *habits* had in many ways preceded Bourdieu, the latter describes *habitus* in its social-psychological aspects less precisely. On the other hand, Bourdieu's description of the social field is much more differentiated. He shows that the communities that make up a modern democracy are characterized by intense struggles about roles and positions of participation. For him, what is at stake in these struggles are, among other things, different versions of capital (such as economic, social, cultural, or symbolic) that represent cultural resources and influences. With regard to Dewey's criteria, Bourdieu's criticism would suggest that the sharing of a diversity of common values and interests within a social group or community is from the very start distorted by power struggles about interests, influences, and positions. Even within any modern democratic social group, we find subdivisions and rivaling movements with different access to cultural capitals that try to secure their own influence through establishing their partly exclusive discourses. For example, in the case of artists and social scientists, especially philosophers, their linguistic *habitus* is often not influential enough to be successful in the general market of opinions, especially in the mass media. This is not only because they tend to think in the abstract, but because cultural capital often resists being profitable in any economic sense. If this is the case, then economic capital underestimates or neglects the value of cultural capital. Therefore, philosophers, artists, or social scientists often cultivate their own very specific discourses and limited counterpublics to survive in society at all.

This situation throws a new light on the role of experts or public intellectuals. At present, the linguistic *habitus* of criticism and cultural theory, as advocated by Dewey, can hardly be said to be an influential position in the field of science, and much less in the general society, the mass media, and the marketplace of globalization. This *habitus* aims to show humans good ways to democracy and gives good reasons and criteria for analyzing culture as a whole and criticizing current ways of living together, but it is only being discussed in relatively small circles of experts with limited public effects. Responding to the observation that nowadays the groups interested in these discourses are becoming smaller, Richard Rorty speaks of a *therapeutic discourse* that has remained for public intellectuals. Rorty interprets this change as a decreasing of effectiveness, especially of the social sciences and humanities. Pragmatists and constructivists have to face this situation. They are hardly in a position to gain much influence in society and the mass media in order to disseminate and realize their "good" ideas.

Rorty's thesis is much debated, but less debatable is the fact that Bourdieu does actually draw attention to a precarious point of participation in scholarship and its language:

> The recognition of the legitimacy of the official language ... is inscribed, in a practical state, in dispositions which are impalpably inculcated, through a long and slow process of acquisition, by the sanctions of the linguistic market, and which are therefore adjusted, without any cynical calculation or consciously experienced constraint, to the chances of material and symbolic profit which the laws of price formation characteristic of a given market objectively offer to the holders of a given linguistic capital. (Bourdieu 1991, 51)

Scientific inquiry, in other words, is as rooted in the context of fields and markets as all other events and objects are. Scholars of the social sciences are themselves part of the objects they investigate, and, as Bourdieu says, they therefore cannot take for granted their own academic competence, nor stake out any claims for a proposed neutral standpoint of truth.

Thus, I conclude, that just like all of the other perspectives in society, science must not only problemize a participatory role but also needs an observer theory that is capable of bearing on existing participations, as well as those that have as yet not been considered. This is basically what Bourdieu does when he differentiates participations and relates them back to the real-life context. In doing so, he speaks of a field in which economic capital, cultural capital, linguistic capital, and social capital—and it would be possible to construct more symbolic capitals here—are all in competition with each other. The description of this competition, as constructed by Bourdieu, helps us create an overview of events and of certain forms of capital that allows us to better understand participation in complex modern societies.

From a constructivist point of view, approaches such as Dewey's or Bourdieu's should be complemented by an explicit observer theory that exposes the multiple descriptions of social reality as constructs. These constructions help us grasp the complexity of our worlds of action and reflect how we achieve them. One of the advantages of acknowledging the constructive development of versions of reality lies in allowing us to recognize the fact that no age has as yet been able to create a complete *knowledge*, and that the very expectation of completeness is illusory in itself. This acknowledgment does not signify arbitrariness or mere relativism, but it points to the precarious starting point of all statements about truth claims. Statements are specific constructions whose truthfulness cannot simply be copied from nature or any object, for statements always exist within the context of observations, participations and actions, which themselves contain requirements that enter into every statement. This even applies to every empirical construction of facts.

In light of the two presented criteria for democracy, for example, there is a long history of observation, partaking, and action that stretches from the constitution of democracy in antiquity to the present day (philosophical links). It refers to a history of law stretching from the law of nature to civil law (legal history). It relates to a history of economic changes, in which the introduction of wage labor went hand in hand with the industrial and democratic revolutions of modernity (economic history). It also relates to a history of women's emancipation, which had to struggle for a long time for recognition within the democratic movements (feminism). And there is a history of symbolic capital if we take the perspective of Bourdieu.

There is no complete list of such histories and preconditions. In the sense of Dewey these are facts that condition human activity, but at the same time they also are facts that have been conditioned by human activity. From a constructivist point of view, we avoid any misunderstanding that any knowledge of facts could be independent from human constructions. We could admit that any construction can become a precondition for further constructions and is itself conditioned by earlier constructions. But Dewey's emphasis on the difference of two separate kinds of facts in the earlier quote seems to allude to a commonsense realism or naturalism—of his and our time—that shows a halfhearted constructivism.

Seen this way, Dewey's two criteria are constructions that have been developed out of a huge context of the actions and experiences of humans that stretches far back in time. To be applied in a viable way, each member of society has to reconstruct them in order to grasp their meaning, reflect on them, and finally to give them new and extended meanings by applying them to all fields of democratic life. They even imply this constructive activity, including the imaginative vision of democracy, in the form of a utopian expectation. They will only be able to be realized if and when the democratically oriented participants can perceive themselves in their roles as observers, who are able to review and imagine their own actions in relation to others and the consequences of democratic interactions on all levels of social life. This power of imagination and reflection will be a basis for them to recognize how far they have advanced in their democratic orientation. Democracy is a way and a process and never a final given.

2.3.2. Introducing a Third Criterion. We found that Dewey's two criteria of democracy in our own time need to be reconstructed and supplemented according to our changed contexts. I now suggest a third criterion that is already implicit in Dewey's approach. To my mind, this third criterion needs more explicit mention and also a somewhat different elaboration in our own time.

First I recall the frame for the two criteria. For Dewey, this is the social function, which he believes to be indispensable for education in democracy. Democracy for him is always primarily a form and perspective of social interaction which, on the one hand, can only be realized once actions actually take place and, on the other, when actions are consciously needed, planned, and appropriately executed. To realize this, we need education. And this, so it seems to me, should be explicitly stated as a criterion for democracy. For Dewey, in his time the necessary connection between democracy and education was still so obvious that it seems hardly surprising that he himself did not explicitly mention it as a third criterion. After having witnessed in the twentieth-century so many educational theories and philosophies that have lost this connection, we today would be well advised to make explicit the constituent role of education for democracy in our theories.

The criterion could read as follows: To make democracy possible, learning must never be confined to but one view of one interpretive community. It must always involve different variations, extensions, and reconstructions of knowledge or imagination within a community of learning, and it must give learners a chance to explore diverse lines and perspectives of observing and acting. Learners must have the possibility to come to know other communities outside of the norms and values they are used to. This possibility must include ways of cross-border communication, understanding, and participation. Such learning will succeed most readily if a democratic community of practice exists and indeed allows for practical partaking of all learners in choosing and constructing contents, relations, and methods of learning. In the degree to which learners in their habitual context of learning are confronted with a rather narrow social and cultural field of experience, measures must be taken to introduce multicultural perspectives and intercultural communication. In a self-reflexive effort, all learners must learn to see themselves—as globally as possible—as observers of their own participation in communities, and of other participations of other humans in other communities. The connecting orientation should be a democratic development whose minimum requirement is to allow all participants—from no matter which community—to live in a pluralistic, diverse, and learning society with a cooperative vision of growth.

To such an approach any kind of fundamentalism is an enemy. That is why a democratic orientation cannot be liberal without qualification, that is, without rejecting anti-democratic principles such as authoritarian dependencies, holy hierarchies, unequal rights, and forms of structurally unjust leadership. It has to fight against those principles wherever they offend democratic living together. However, such delimitations themselves are historical battlegrounds around specific interpretations of democracy.

The third criterion states more precisely that democracy cannot exist without being learned time and again in and through democratic ways of life. Democracy is always simultaneously a cognitive, social, imaginative, and emotional construct. It needs to be learned if it is to be effective. The danger for democratically oriented societies of losing this orientation increases proportionally to the societies' decreasing willingness to invest in such learning.

The third criterion does not at all ensure that democracy will sufficiently succeed. Dewey already knew that democracy has to be seen as a process, and a great emphasis for him lay on learning, in order to provide everyone with a chance to participate and succeed in the struggle for participation in democratic rights. But as the time since Dewey has shown, even democratically oriented states are not able to perform this task adequately in equal measure. Learning is always interlocked in the battles for positions, as Bourdieu describes, for example, in his *Homo Academicus* (1988). Learning creates differences, as Bourdieu proves (1990, 1993), because learning is situated within the contexts of generating symbolic forms of capital. Learning creates at least a different cultural and social capital, which has to prove itself in the various markets of the globalized world, and which is in no way equally distributed to all humans. In this situation, one of the most promising chances for democracy lies in the following: to counterbalance current inequalities in societies at least in terms of equal access to learning, and partly to compensate the injustices of unequal advancement. Learning must be supportive for all learners but must especially help those learners who start from a context of disadvantage or discrimination. Learners must be allowed to take relatively equal chances to act and to partake in contexts of learning as a prerequisite to participating in social life. Only societies that support and develop this intention on a broad and generous scale express a willingness toward lived democracy, for only such a willingness manifests a general societal interest in a democratic orientation that goes beyond mere paying of lip service combined with the securing of existing vested rights, thus letting the rich get richer and the poor poorer. A democratic togetherness of responsibility, and chances for development in the field of learning, may not lead to an all-encompassing equality, but at least it does not defeat all of the opportunities from the outset.

This was a matter of course in Dewey's thinking, but for our times, in the face of the development of the school systems, we need to highlight it as a declared criterion. We do so in order to fill our constructs of learning for democracy with content and meaning appropriate to our own time.

3. Democratic Education and the Need for a Democratic School System

Finally, I return once again to my example of the tripartite secondary school system in Germany, mentioned earlier. It can be shown that the attendant form of selection of pupils, which comes from the old Prussian class privilege, not only follows a tradition rooted in old-class notions but also fundamentally violates the three criteria suggested.

The first criterion is violated because not all of the participants in this education will be able to receive the best possible prospects of attendance and development. The mere idea that more talented children are distinguished from less talented ones by institutional selection, and through constraint to restricted paths of development through grouping and assignment starting at the age of ten, conflicts with Dewey's concern.[15] Dewey himself always fought for a comprehensive school type, which aims at involving and engaging pupils in a long, shared time of mutual enrichment and encouragement. This is a development process in which they are able to interact and profit from each other's abilities and opportunities. More advanced pupils can help weaker ones. Everyone has the chance to achieve and to make successes in learning, dependent on his or her abilities. Contrary to this, it has been and still is being argued in the German discussion that this would, in the first place, harm the more talented pupils. This statement is rarely critically questioned but rather further substantiated by references to the supposedly successful selection system. Yet international school comparisons like Program for International Student Assessment (PISA) have recently shown that German schools by no means fulfill what is officially claimed.[16] Comprehensive school systems have proven to be more successful. School systems operating according to Dewey's first criterion are more successful particularly because they do not equate difference with narrow boundaries and selection variants (at far too young an age) but in contrast enable all adolescents, over the course of a relatively long period of time, to progress at their own pace. This takes possible late development into account, while at the same time respecting the general diversity and dissimilarity of abilities. Heterogeneity (i.e., the growth of differences) in this perspective does not constitute a handicap but an essential chance and resource for better individual success for all learners. International teaching and educational research, therefore, repeatedly exposes heterogeneous learning groups as a successful model.

Considering international comparisons, being a pupil in Germany nowadays comes close to a kind of punishment. While in other comparably developed countries 90 percent of the pupils switch to a higher school level after completing comprehensive school and 70 percent of them pass the Abitur[17] (e.g., in Sweden), Germany, with only 30 percent of its pupils passing the Abitur, only ranks in the lower third of all developed countries, and continues to fall behind. The Organization for Economic Co-operation and Development (OECD) has reprimanded this repeatedly. If one does not want to follow the thesis of Germans being genetically more thickheaded than people from comparable countries, then consequently the responsibility must be attributed to the educational and school system that makes insufficient use of its learners' abilities. So much for the first criterion.

But it is with regard to the second criterion, to my mind, that the German situation appears most problematic. The selection and rigid separation of the German school system has the negative effect that children and young adults from socially deprived families as well as from families of immigrants are accumulated in the lower segment of the school system. Their educational prospects are thus spoiled at quite an early stage. This produces mind-sets entertaining notions of "those up there" and "those down there" that constrict a cross-border communication and debate between social groups. In the long run, this also creates rather poor prerequisites for democratic advancement. It furthers the formation of a deep social division, which will cause follow-up costs and political consequences that cannot as yet be foreseen. According to Dewey, given such a constellation, we have to fear for the development of democracy itself.

On the whole, the third criterion I have set up is violated by the fact that learning and education are not widely enough recognized as basic societal opportunities. The growth of the learners is split along institutional boarding lines that define rather closed fields of positions. In the long run this also hampers societal growth. However, in my opinion, the central task of all industrialized societies in the next decades of an increasingly globalized age will be to appreciate learning qualifications as an essential capital, as a crucial resource for further societal development. This capital will be the essential raw and basic material of a late industrial and cultural development, which we also need to regard as a relevant basis for the requirements for the development of democracy. If, on the other hand, the separation of social groups is increased by a selective education and an increasingly unequal access to learning, then democracy itself will be threatened in its credibility.

The fact that it is possible even today to describe and reflect problems and opportunities for development in education and democracy by using and extending Dewey's criteria shows how current Dewey's thinking continues to be. This has not only a theoretical kind of relevance useful for discussions in the theoretical ivory tower of academia, but it is also of practical, challenging, current-day relevance. It may motivate all of those for whom democracy is not merely a word that stands for materialistic security and a convenient life. It may remind us to view the richness of democracy in its diversity of approaches to life, in the creativity of a culture and its products, and in the solidarity between all participants. Democracy—as a reflection on Dewey's criteria shows—is an imagination and intention that still may give us great hope for the possible growth of individuals *and* the growth of cultures.

Notes

1. The translation by Erich Hylla was published in Breslau (Ferdinand Hirt). It was edited without alterations by Jürgen Oelkers and republished by Beltz in 1993. To comprehend Dewey's work, the given translation is not sufficient, especially because it has not been revised with regard to the present state of Dewey scholarship.

2. For more on habits, customs, and traditions, see Neubert's chapter in this book. For more on habits, impulses, and growth, see Jim Garrison's chapter in this book.

3. Dewey uses the term *habit* (compare MW 14). This refers not only to a practice of pure behavior but also indicates an attitude of interpreting the world. This comes close to the term *habitus* as used by Bourdieu.

4. At least in Dewey's political works, and particularly in his late work, we can detect a number of passages that present Dewey as a thinker who did not examine the family isolated from its context and the fractures of the age. Nevertheless, sometimes we can perceive in Dewey's approach an overall tendency toward the idealization of American social institutions with a certain standard of prosperity that he sets as a general target perspective or as a horizon for his notions of society. Yet we also need to consider the many passages where he criticizes the cultural and social aspects of American society.

5. With regard to this issue, compare also as a comprehensive debate Campbell (1992) and more recently his chapter in this book. Compare further Neubert's contribution to this book.

6. One of the few German works dealing with this phenomenon was written by Bohnsack (1976). For the current discussion and fur-

ther literature references, compare in particular Hickman, Neubert, and Reich (2004).

7. Compare to the chapters of Judith Green, Jim Garrison, and Charlene Haddock Seigfried in this book.

8. These objections are made from the perspective of the theory of interactionist constructivism, as, for instance, presented by Reich (1998a, 1998b, 2002, 2004), Neubert (1998), and Hickman, Neubert, and Reich (2004).

9. Charlene Haddock Seigfried (1996) reconstructs Dewey to develop a pragmatist feminism. She can show some blind spots too.

10. From the spectrum of Bauman's works, compare in particular 1987, 1993, 1997, 2000, 2001.

11. This refers for interactive constructivism to a possible wide spectrum of theories, affiliated with Foucault, cultural studies, Laclau and Mouffe, and others. But also in pragmatism we find good references. Compare for the German discussions Jörke (2003).

12. From a constructivist perspective, this quest appears to be needless anyway (cf. Reich in Burckhart and Reich 2000).

13 As an introduction, compare also Neubert and Reich (2001).

14. For a more complex reconstruction of pragmatism and community and the role of experts, compare, for example, Bernstein (1998).

15. And not only with his concern but also with the results of modern teaching and educational research. Should anyone feel that this is still insufficient, it also conflicts with the empirical data collected in internationally conducted school comparisons that now relentlessly pinpoint the weaknesses of the German school system. This has as yet not led to any visible school reforms. Rather, German politicians try to escape responsibility by pursuing a strategy that leaves the structural roots untouched, because the imagination, which is needed for potential changes, despairs of the past's formation of habits sounding like an anxious "Dwell on...."

16. A criticism of the German school system from an international perspective can be found, for example, in Schnepf (2002).

17. A-level or school-leaving examination at grammar school needed for entry to higher education.

Works Cited

Bauman, Z. 1987. *Legislators and interpreters: On modernity, post-modernity, and intellectuals.* Cambridge: Polity Press.

———. 1993. *Postmodern ethics.* Oxford: Basil Blackwell.

———. 1997. *Postmodernity and its discontents.* Cambridge: Polity Press.

———. 2000. *Liquid modernity.* Cambridge: Polity Press.

———. 2001. *The individualized society.* Cambridge: Polity Press.

Bernstein, R. J. 1998. Community in the pragmatic tradition. In *The revival of pragmatism,* ed. M. Dickstein, Durham, NC, and London: Duke University Press.

Bohnsack, F. 1976. *Erziehung zur Demokratie. John Dewey's Pädagogik und ihre Bedeutung für die Reform unserer Schule.* Ravensburg: Maier.

Bourdieu, P. 1988. *Homo academicus.* Cambridge: Polity Press.

———. 1990. *The logic of practice.* Cambridge: Polity Press.

———. 1991. *Language and symbolic power.* Cambridge, MA: Harvard University Press.

———. 1993. *The field of cultural production.* Cambridge: Polity Press.

Campbell, J. 1992. *The community reconstructs: The meaning of pragmatic social thought.* Urbana: University of Illinois Press.

———. 1998. Dewey's conception of community. In *Reading Dewey: Interpretations for a postmodern generation,* ed. L. Hickman, Bloomington: Indiana University Press, 23–42.

Green, J. 1999. *Deep democracy: Community, diversity, and transformation.* New York: Rowman & Littlefield.

Hickman, L., Neubert, S., and Reich, K. 2004. *John Dewey: Zwischen Pragmatismus und Konstruktivismus: Reihe: Interaktionistischer Konstruktivismus.* Münster: Waxmann.

Jörke, D. 2003. *Demokratie als Erfahrung: John Dewey und die politische Philosophie der Gegenwart.* Wiesbaden: Westdeutscher Verlag.

Mouffe, C. 1994. *The return of the political.* London: Verso.

———. 1996. *Deconstruction and pragmatism.* New York: Routledge.

Neubert, S. 1998. Erkenntinis, Verhalten und Kommunikation: John Deweys Philosophie des "experience" in interaktionistisch-konstruktivistischer Interpretation. Münster u.a.: Waxmann.

Neubert, S., and K. Reich. 2001. The ethnocentric view: Constructivism and the practice of intercultural discourse. In *Learning for the future: Proceedings of the learning conference*, ed. B. Cope and M. Kalantzis, Australia: Common Ground Publishing.

Reich, K. 1998a. *Die Ordnung der Blicke: Perspektiven des interaktionistisch Konstruktivismus Band 1: Beobachtung und die Unschärfen der Erkenntnis*. Neuwied u.a.: Luchterhand.

———. 1998b. Die Ordnung der Blicke: *Band 2: Beziehungen und Lebenswelt*. Neuwied u.a.: Luchterhand.

———. 2000. Interaktionistisch-konstruktive Kritik einer universalitischen Begruendung von Ethik und Moral" In *Begründung von Moral: Diskursethik versus Konstruktivismus eine Streitschrift*, ed. H. Burckhart and K. Reich, Würzburg: Könighausen und Neumann, 88–181.

———. 2002. *Systemisch-konstruktivistische Pädagogik: Einführung in Grundlagen einer Interktionistisch-konstruktivischen Pädagogik*. Neuwied u.a.: Luchterhand.

———. 2004. *Konstruktivistische Didaktik*. Neuwied u.a.: Luchterhand.

Rousseau, J. J. [1761] 1988. *The social contract*. Buffalo, N.Y.: Prometheus Books.

———. [1762] 1979. *Emile*. New York: Basic Books.

Schnepf, S. V. 2002. A sorting hat that fails?: The transition from primary to secondary school in Germany. Innocenti Working Paper No. 92. Florence: UNICEF Innocenti Research Center, http://www.unicef-icdc.org/publications.

Seigfried, C. H. 1996. *Pragmatism and feminism: Reweaving the social fabric*. Chicago: University of Chicago Press.

Thompson, J. B. 1991. Introduction. In *Language and symbolic power*, ed. P. Bourdieu, Cambridge: Harvard University Press, 1–31.

Chapter 4

Dewey's Pluralism Reconsidered— Pragmatist and Constructivist Perspectives on Diversity and Difference

Stefan Neubert

John Dewey's philosophy is a pluralistically oriented approach. The centrality of pluralist thinking is one major trait that makes his pragmatism so attractive for present-day constructivists. His pluralism is not restricted to his political theory and vision of democracy but is rooted in his generous understanding of human experience as rich, diversified, resourceful, and abundant in meanings. His repeated and forceful comments on themes such as qualitative individuality, originality, creativity, and incommensurability as inextinguishable traits of experience, his insistence on the necessity of taking into account the vague, obscure, and twilight phases of existence, and his frequent reminder that we always have to inquire into concrete and unique situations as providing touchstones for our judgments and beliefs all testify to the genuine pluralism that is at the very heart of his philosophy.

In what follows, I first elaborate briefly on the role that pluralism plays in Dewey's general philosophical outlook.[1] I especially focus on some of the roots of pluralist thinking in his basic philosophical concept of experience (1.1) and turn briefly to some implications of pluralism in his political thought (1.2). In a second step, I ask what use we, today, can make of Dewey's philosophical pluralism, given the changes and developments that distinguish our own situation from the constellations of Dewey's lifetime. I highlight three possible lines of reconstruction that I think can be helpful for Deweyans to move forward (and partly beyond Dewey) in a productive way. These lines concern Dewey's ideas about three central and closely related questions: (2.1) What is the meaning of social progress and how is it related to scientific methods? (2.2) What forms of social control are appropriate for the regulation of social interactions? (2.3) What influence do social interests and power relations have on the development of democratic communications? Regarding each of these topics, I think that from a perspective of today a critical reading can detect a certain tension or ambiguity in Dewey's writings. I suggest that we can make productive use of this tension if we distinguish between those aspects of his approach that can best help us rethink the challenges and implications of pluralism for our own time and other aspects of his thought that reflect influential ideas of his time but seem no longer appropriate or convincing today. Along the way, I indicate some theoretical perspectives from the Köln Interactive Constructivism program that may be helpful for the necessary reconstruction work.[2]

1.0. Experience, Experimentalism, and the Necessity of Context

Dewey has elaborated on the rich and inexhaustible diversity of meanings lived in the concrete life experiences of humans in many comprehensive and subtle studies. One may only think of the extensive body of his writings, for example, in the fields of social psychology (MW 14), theory of education (MW 9), philosophy of communication (LW 1: 132 ff.), theory of art (LW 10), and political philosophy (e.g., LW 2: 235 ff.; LW 11: 1 ff.; LW 13: 63 ff.) that constitutes a resourceful and multilayered cultural theory that is highly suggestive to the present day. Basic to his philosophical pluralism is the rejection of the idea of a uniform or universal faculty of reason underlying all human inquiries—be it in the sense of some transcendental source or of an empirical entity. His plea for "experience" as the starting point of all philosophical reflection is a plea to address our world experimentally as an open universe that allows for an inexhaustible abundance of possible perspectives and interpretations. He rejects the traditional notion of reason "as the highest organ or 'faculty' for laying hold on ultimate truths" and suggests that we use the more contemporary word "intelligence" instead—not as something ready-made but as "a shorthand designation for great and ever-growing methods of observation, experiment, and reflective reasoning" (MW 12: 258). Intelligence, for Dewey, is something that has been developed out of human experiences in a long process of cultural history.[3] Accordingly, it does not primarily designate an individual possession but a quality of human inquiries carried out by communities of interpreters. Dewey treats theory not as an end in itself but as instrumental: Theoretical formulations are hypotheses for conducting further inquiries, based on observation, that put theory to experimental test. The primacy of experimentalism against any claim to an allegedly superior or ultimate access to knowledge is essential to Dewey's idea of intelligence.

From this standpoint, knowledge always presupposes interaction and communication. Inquiry is primarily a social affair that does not only allow for, but depends on, a plurality of perspectives brought to bear on the problems at hand. And it is important to see that diversity of perspectives is a starting point for Dewey, not a somewhat undesirable situation to be overcome or dialectically "resolved" by philosophical reasoning. His call to take "the Social" as "the Inclusive Philosophic Idea" (LW 3: 41–54) clearly calls on us to welcome the multitude of standpoints, interests, interpretations, and values implied in social experience as necessary resources for thought. According to Dewey, "the Social," in all of its diversity, is the most genuine subject matter for philosophical reflection. He does not tire of warning us against what Raymond Boisvert (1992, 193) calls the philosophical "ideal of asepsis." The most refined and unified products of inquiry, such as scientific or philosophic concepts, must eventually be brought back upon primary experience in all of its coarseness and crudity for experimental testing. Dewey's rejection of the philosophic search for absolute certainties, eternal and immutable truths, is a clear consequence of his profoundly experimentalist approach. For him, the implicit diversity of meanings found in lived experience is the primary context of philosophical method. It cannot be disposed of by any form of unity reached through theory and reflection. Taking "experience"—"the last inclusive context" of our interactions in and with our world—as the "basis and terminus of philosophy" (MW 6: 20), Dewey insists that we abandon the old philosophical habit of identifying reality with our systems or objects of knowledge. He thinks that existence is characterized by an ineradicable mixture of the precarious and the stable (see LW 1: 42 ff.). Stability means that we can make observations and construct theories that allow for order and orientation. But no matter how sophisticated and refined our systems of knowledge may be, we cannot get rid of the precarious phase of our experience. Contingency and ambiguity are genuine traits of life that cannot be explained away by philosophic theory. The obscure and vague remain with us. Belief and knowledge are necessarily surrounded by a context of ambiguous meanings from which they emerge through inquiry. Lived experience is much richer in potential meanings than any symbolic system can ever expose. "What is really 'in' experience extends much further than that which at any time is *known*" (LW 1: 27, emphasis in the original). It is important to note that from the standpoint of knowledge objects must be distinct, and their meanings must be explicitly defined. "But it is equally important to note that the dark and twilight abound" (27 ff.). For Dewey, any object of primary experience has potential meanings and implications that are not yet made explicit. Any act has factors that are hidden. "Strain thought as far as we may and not all consequences can be foreseen or made an express or known part of reflection and decision" (28).

Speaking more systematically, then, Dewey's philosophical pluralism is deeply rooted in his philosophical core concepts "experience" and "inquiry." Human "experience" implies a cultural diversity of standpoints, interests, interpretations, and values. It contains an abundance of potential meanings that cannot be reduced to one single perspective. Experience is more comprehensive than any system of cognition or interpretation. It "stretches" beyond the limits of the known. "Inquiry" is of necessity partial and selective. To call it "experimental" is but to acknowledge that the underlying tension between "the precarious" and "the stable" allows for no wholesale resolution. We can never completely exhaust, resolve, or "stabilize" the potential implications of experienced situations. We must remain open for new and unexpected experiences that may lead to new and unexpected interpretations. To create and promote "a respect for concrete human experience and its potentialities" (LW 1: 41), philosophy must of necessity take a pluralistic stance.

For Dewey, this implies that we take the idea of context more seriously than philosophers often did in the past. He exposed and summarized his ideas about contextualism in a lecture delivered in Berkeley in 1931 and published under the title "Context and Thought" (LW 6: 3 ff.). There he concludes that the "significance of 'experience' for philosophic method is . . . but the acknowledgement of the indispensability of context in thinking when that recognition is carried to its full term" (20). To carry it to its full term means that we recognize the contextuality of all of our observations and interpretations, even if it is impossible for us to explicitly expose all relevant contexts at any given moment. In our normal experience context, to a large extent, is just there. We take it for granted. We do not think about it unless some part of it becomes problematic, because we are confronted with a new, unexpected situation. As humans we inhabit our world by habits formed in the intercourse with a natural and cultural environment. Habit means that our experiences are pervaded by a temporal and spatial background (11 ff.)—the diachronic and synchronic contexts of history and culture implicit in all of our observations and interpretations. Language and the use of symbols are powerful contexts that pervade our every thought (4 ff.).[4] "Traditions are ways of interpretation and of observation, of valuation, of everything explicitly thought of. They are the circumambient atmosphere which thought must breathe; no one ever had an idea except as he inhaled some of this atmosphere" (12). According to Dewey, we also have to take the more "subjective" phases of context into account. All of our observations and interpretations imply what he calls "selective interests" (14 ff.), that is, the desires, motives, and predilections by which we choose and distinguish, for example, the relevant from the irrelevant. "Every particular case of thinking is what it is because of some attitude" (14 ff.)—and be it the attitude of being "objective" in thinking. Without this phase of subjectivity, there would be neither individuality nor originality in thought.[5]

Now the cultural contexts of our experiences supplied by language, traditions, habits, and selective interests are resources as well as limitations. They provide us with the necessary tools for acting and thinking, but they also hold us captives so that we often become oblivious about context and take it as a matter of course. In everyday life this forgetfulness, for the most part, does no harm and is, indeed, unavoidable. But Dewey thinks that there are specific dangers for philosophy that arise from neglect or ignoring of context. "I should venture to assert that the most pervasive fallacy of philosophic thinking goes back to neglect of context" (5). Dewey specifically mentions two "counterpart" fallacies in this connection that match each other, in that they both tend to collapse pluralism into a monistic scheme of explanation. The "analytic fallacy" consists in dissolving reality into distinct and isolated elements that are then treated not as results constructed within the contexts of inquiry but as something final and independent, as the really real, the original constituents out of which reality is made up (6 ff.). The "fallacy of unlimited universalization" is found "when it is asserted...that the goal of thinking, particularly of philosophic thought, is to bring all things whatsoever into a single coherent and all inclusive whole" (8). In both cases, neglect (or even denial) of context is harmful, because it involves forgetfulness of the limiting conditions of philosophic inquiry. It therefore violates an important principle of every pluralist approach—the relatedness of specific perspectives to specific contexts and thus the limitedness and incompleteness of any perspective that we take. William James's famous pluralist credo, that "neither the whole of truth nor the whole of good is revealed to any single observer" (James, 1958, 88 ff.), sounds in the background of Dewey's much more sober formulation: "Within the limits of context found in any valid inquiry, 'reality' thus means the confirmed outcome, actual or potential, of the inquiry that is undertaken.... When 'reality' is sought for at large, it is without intellectual import" (LW 6: 8 ff.). Although context can never be completely penetrated and made explicit by reflection, acknowledgment of the limits of context, Dewey suggests, can teach us philosophic "humility" and prevent us from "a too unlimited and dogmatic universalization" of our conclusions. "[We] would not freeze the quotidian truths relevant to the problems that emerge in [our] own background of culture into eternal truths inherent in the very nature of things" (13).

1.1. Plural Democracy

Dewey's philosophical pluralism is of course not restricted to his theories about experience, inquiry, and knowledge. Most significantly, it pervades his ethical and political thought and his vision of democracy. His view of modern society is clearly pluralistic and multicultural. For example, he writes in *Democracy and Education*, "Such words as 'society' and 'community' are likely to be misleading, for they have a tendency to make us think there is single thing corresponding to the single word. As a matter of fact, a modern society is many societies more or less loosely connected" (MW 9: 25). And he goes on to argue that while in former times societies were "comparatively homogeneous," the developments of "commerce, transportation, intercommunication, and emigration" have brought about cultural diversity as a characteristic, indispensable trait of modern society (25). Upon the whole, Dewey suggests that this diversity enriches democracy. Although it must be "balanced" and its "centrifugal forces" must be "counteracted" (26) (e.g., by means of democratic institutions such as the public school), it multiplies the cultural resources necessary for solving the complex problems and challenges of modern societies.

Basic to the democratic way of life, therefore, is the recognition and appreciation of differences. Dewey's two main criteria of a democratic community (see MW 9: 89), "How numerous and varied are the interests which are consciously shared? How full and free is the interplay with other forms of association?", clearly point to the recognition of differences within social groups as well as between one social group and another. And he leaves no doubt that for him this recognition is not only a matter of benevolent tolerance but also a personally educative element of democratic communication. For example, he writes in his late essay "Creative Democracy—The Task Before Us," "To cooperate by giving differences a chance to show themselves because of the belief that the expression of difference is not only a right of the other persons but is a means of enriching one's own life-experience, is inherent in the democratic personal way of life" (LW 14: 228). The democratic principle of equality, he insists, implies that we acknowledge "the incommensurable" (i.e., the otherness of others) "in a world in which an existence must be reckoned with on its own account, not as something capable of equation with and transformation into something else" (MW 11: 53). Democratic communication presupposes that all members, groups, or communities have the right and opportunity not only to participate in public deliberation and decision making but also to speak for themselves and be heard on their own behalf. This principle is essential to Dewey's radical notion of democracy. It also is one key to his model of education, which insists that we give all learners the opportunity to participate actively, constructively, and responsively in the organization of their learning and be recognized in their differences of background, history, needs, desires, motifs, and interests.

2. Social Intelligence Revisited

The growing international Dewey scholarship since the early 1980s shows that his philosophy in many respects still speaks to us as a powerful and resourceful tool of cultural interpretation and reconstruction. It would be no exaggeration to say that in many respects Dewey is still a timely thinker for us.[6] But of course like all of us, Dewey was first of all a child of his own time. Accordingly, intertwined in his overall approach, there are also a number of ideas and expectations characteristic of his own age that may appear today, in the first decade of a new century, as restricted or partly even outmoded. After all, it should not take us by surprise that some of the ideas that have been influential among intellectuals at the beginning of the twentieth-century—for example, ideas emanating from the movement of American progressivism, of which Dewey was an intimate participant—have now lost part of their suggestive power. The challenge for Deweyans today is to try to make the best and most productive use of Dewey's approach for our own time. If we find that this task demands of us to abandon some of his ideas that do not seem appropriate any longer, or to broaden and revisit other of his views in order to overcome certain internal restrictions, we should not hesitate to do so. There is nothing un-Deweyan in reconstructing Dewey, even if such reconstruction entails that in some respects we "pass Dewey by" (cf. Gavin 2003). After all, he himself taught us that lesson when he reminded us that philosophy must always be prepared to reconstruct its own concepts and views with regard to the changing sociocultural contexts of its time. And this often implies that ideas once prevalent and suggestive no longer appeal to us as urgent or convincing. For example, he wrote in *The Need for a Recovery of Philosophy* that intellectual "advance" at times involves that "[m]en's minds grow cold to their former intellectual concerns; ideas that were burning fade; interests that were urgent seem remote" (MW 10: 3). And in *The Influence of Darwinism on Philosophy* he claims that "intellectual progress usually occurs through sheer abandonment of questions...an abandonment that results from their decreasing vitality and a change of urgent interest. We do not solve them: We get over them. Old questions are solved by disappearing, evaporating, while new questions corresponding to the changed attitude of endeavour and preference take their place" (MW 4: 14).

In what follows, I wish to briefly discuss three possible lines of reconstruction that may help us overcome what, from today's perspective, may appear as some internal delimitations of Dewey's overall pluralist approach. With regard to all three themes, I think that helpful suggestions for the necessary reconstruction work can already be found in Dewey's writings, although they are sometimes overshadowed by influential predilections of his time that narrowed some of his views and prevented him from elaborating others to full extent. But rather than charging Dewey with inconsistency, I think that we should see this ambivalence as a sign of the depth and richness of his thought that dived deeply into his time and moved way ahead in an attempt to anticipate future developments. We may today make productive use of the tension that necessarily resulted from this venture.

2.1. Social Progress and "The Scientific Method"

Dewey wrote at a time when the triumphant progress of the "scientific revolution" was for many observers still so obvious and unambiguous that the imagination of unprecedented social progress attendant to it had still much of the intemperate suggestive power it was to lose in the second half of the twentieth-century. Science had indeed revolutionized social practices in almost every field of daily life to an extent that it seemed self-evident for many progressive intellectuals to bet the hope for further social progress on the extension of application of the "scientific method" to the solution of human problems on an ever-growing scale. These social expectations about "Science and Progress" were embedded in a strong, influential metanarrative of modernity that was largely taken for granted by many. If we review Dewey's position in this context from the temporal distance of today, a close reading provides a rather multilayered picture of his attitudes toward social progress, science, and methods that calls for a critical as well as a constructive interpretation.

Social Progress. Of course Dewey's philosophy cannot be understood without the cultural background of American progressivism. He actively participated over his long lifetime in many progressive movements of the period (see Westbrook 1991). Westbrook's phrase "progressive democracy" indeed expresses Dewey's political project quite well (115 ff.). Seen from a (post)modern perspective of today, many early twentieth-century narratives of "progress" (e.g., in the way of peace, prosperity, technological control, socialism, and other topics) used a rhetoric that suggested a rather unqualified and exaggerated optimism about the prospects of the twentieth-century. And also in Dewey's writings, one finds formulations where the social reformer in him waxes enthusiastic with expectations of unprecedented social advancements. It is easy, therefore, to mis-interpret Dewey as a simple, uncritical believer in "progress." But his ideas about the meaning of progressivism—or what he himself sometimes aptly called "meliorism"—were upon the whole more complex than that. There are many places where he reflects deeply into the ambiguous and contradictory experiences he himself had over his lifetime with the ideas of social reconstruction and social progress. Books such as *Experience and Nature* (LW 1) testify to his comprehensive and sensitive understanding of the past history of Western culture and thought. He repeatedly warned his contemporaries against too-simple, naive ideas about "progress" as something that will come with historical necessity and ease. His deep philosophical understanding of the meaning of contingency gave him an acute sense of the precarious, complex, and inherently difficult nature of all social developments. For example, in a 1916 essay—when the First World War was already raging in Europe—Dewey defends the idea of "social progress" for which the scientific, industrial, and democratic revolutions had furnished the opportunity. But he also self-critically comments on some unrealistic expectations that he and others had held in the earlier period: "If we have been living in a fools' paradise, in a dream of automatic uninterrupted progress, it is well to be awakened.... For there can be no blinking the fact that much of that faith was childish and irresponsible. We confused rapidity of change with advance, and we took certain gains in our own comfort and ease as signs that cosmic forces were working inevitably to improve the whole state of human affairs" (MW 10: 234 ff.; cf. also MW 14: 197 ff., LW 14: 112 ff.). And, in a book such as *The Public and Its Problems* (LW 2: 235–372), in which he forcefully expresses his democratic meliorism, Dewey also is quite clear about the fact that in modern societies every social advancement involves new complexities and brings with it new and extended problems to be solved.

Despite these qualifications, however, it seems to me that the underlying cultural metanarrative of progressivism carried some "leftovers of nineteenth-century historiography" into Dewey's thought, as Raymond Boisvert critically observes (2003, 95).[7] Among other things, this historiography suggests a

clear-cut progression in human history from an undeveloped or
a "primitive" to an advanced or a "civilized" state of culture,
combined with implicit claims about the superiority of
Western civilization. Seen from todays perspective, the underlying binary is problematic, because it tends to reduce the variety of cultures into one hierarchical schema. Disciplines such
as anthropology, linguistics, history, ethnology, sociology or
cultural studies have done much to abandon such simple
schemata in the twentieth-century because of their subject-
matter's complexity and the colonialist implications that
accompanied the older views (see, e.g., Hall 1992b). They
have, upon the whole, adopted more decidedly pluralist
approaches to culture, language, and symbolic representations
(see, e.g., Hall 1997).

To my mind, Dewey's thinking about cultural history is at
times reminiscent of this nineteenth-century historiography,
which pervaded large parts of the anthropology of his day.
Traces of it appear for example, in the plain contrast between
"savagery" and "civilization" that he repeatedly draws on in his
account of the function of education given in the first four
chapters of his 1916 *Democracy and Education* (see MW 9: 10,
21, 41).[8] On the other hand, there is evidence that he increasingly emancipated himself, especially in his later period, from
these implicit "leftovers." After all, he was a philosopher who
often reconstructed himself over his long lifetime, and his
thinking about the diversity and incommensurability of cultures
seems to have matured considerably in correlation to his own
growing transcultural experiences. His long and extended jour-
neys after the First World War (e.g., to Japan, China, the Soviet
Union, Turkey, and Mexico; see Dykhuizen 1973; Westbrook
1991) particularly may have provided an important background
for this move. For instance, his 1934 book, *Art as Experiences*
(LW 10), combines a pervading cultural criticism of American
civilization and its underlying capitalist order with a deep
respect for the cultural and artistic achievements of other and
heterogeneous cultures. It shows an extraordinary appreciation
for cultural diversity and represents a mature expression of
Dewey's cosmopolitan orientation that clearly points toward a
global and transcultural vision of democracy.

Science and Methods. Dewey was a lifelong advocate of the emancipation powers of the "scientific method" as a general means for social reconstruction and an instrument for "progress." He distinguishes between science as an attitude or a method and science as a body of knowledge or subject matter (see LW 13: 271 ff.). While the latter is an important instrument and an indispensable precondition for solving complex problems in a complex world, the former is even more important from the educational and democratic point of view. Dewey often uses "science" as a short-term phrase for social intelligence based on inquiry and communication, and he thinks that a broader social application of the scientific attitude and method is the safest way we have to more intelligent and more democratic forms of participation and decision making (see 273). In this connection, it is important to bear in mind that Dewey—like classical pragmatism in general—maintains an alternative notion of "science" as compared to the mainstream twentieth-century philosophy of science (cf. Caspary 2000, 45 ff.).[9] Whereas the mainstream positivist notion separates "pure" science from application and holds to a copy theory of knowledge as an ascertained body of facts, Dewey's understanding of the "scientific method" refers first of all to the constructive processes of solving problems through inquiry and the intelligent testing of hypotheses. It has a prospective orientation toward the creation of new phenomena and new hypotheses in response to actually experienced difficulties. The scientific attitude "is rooted in the problems that are set and questions that are raised by the conditions of actuality" (LW 13: 273). For Dewey, knowledge about "facts" is a constructed by-product of experimental problem solving, not something "pure" or complete in itself. And it is most important that such problem solving does not only take place in "science" as a specialized field of inquiry but primarily in the complex, everyday affairs of life that require intelligent solutions: "...the scientific attitude as here conceived," he writes, "is a quality that is manifested in any walk of life.... On its negative side, it is freedom from control by routine, prejudice, dogma, unexamined tradition, sheer self-interest. Positively, it is the will to inquire, to examine, to discriminate, and to draw conclusions only on the basis of evidence after taking pains to gather all available evidence. It is the intention to reach beliefs, and to test those that are entertained, on the basis of observed fact, recognizing also that facts are without meaning save as they point to ideas. It is, in turn, the experimental attitude which recognizes that while ideas are necessary to deal with facts, yet they are working hypotheses to be tested by the consequences they produce" (273). In short, the scientific attitude expresses for Dewey first of all a powerful cultural instrument for construction and criticism (see LW 5: 125 ff.) that can help us invent intelligent methods and find intelligent solutions for the diverse and changing difficulties we have to face as citizens of a modern democratic society. Like democracy itself, it represents an ideal of social intelligence that needs continual development and reconstruction in practice. It is not in the first place an already established practice that can serve as a ready-made and uniform model.

However, Dewey's praise of the social values implied in "the scientific method" gave many readers the impression that he wished to superimpose one fixed set of procedures—namely, the methods that had proven successful in the natural sciences—to all fields of human problem solving alike. In light of the paradigmatic role that the natural sciences played within the early twentieth-century narrative of "Science and Progress," it is easy to understand that, to many readers, Dewey seemed to suggest that there is *one* methodology that equally applies to all fields of human affairs. In addition, Dewey may indeed be charged that he did not always sufficiently qualify his views on this point. But there are several places where he clearly explains that this was not what he meant. Contrary to any form of methodological monism, Dewey had a keen sense of the necessary and reciprocal interdependence between methods and subject matters. For example, in one of his late essays on the future role of philosophy, he italicized the word "methods" in a passage dealing with the development of methods of inquiry into human conditions and added the following footnote that shows that he knew he had often been misunderstood on this point: "The word 'methods' is italicized as a precaution against a possible misunderstanding which would be contrary to what is intended. What is needed is not the carrying over of procedures that have approved themselves in physical science, but *new* methods as adapted to *human* issues and problems, as methods already in scientific use have shown themselves to be in physical subject matter" (LW 16: 379, emphasis is original.).

This insistence on the necessary correlation between methods and subject matters—a point that Dewey also made very clear, for example, in his writings about education and learning (see MW 9)—is a direct consequence of his intense and subtle elaboration of the interdependence between means and ends (see, e.g., LW 13: 226 ff.). It points to a methodological pluralism that takes his insights into the "indispensability of context" seriously. From this standpoint, Dewey's experimentalism implies that we time and again have to construct, deconstruct, and reconstruct our methods with regard to the concrete problems and situations we have to deal with. This is true for science and philosophy as well as for all other fields of human problem solving. The new can only be created on the basis of a partial deconstruction of old methods and beliefs (cf. MW 12: 262 ff.).[10] And significantly, despite his alleged prepossession with the natural sciences, Dewey expects in 1930 that a new movement in philosophy "will emerge when the *significance of the social sciences and arts* has become an object of reflective attention in the same way that mathematical and physical sciences have been made the objects of thought in the past, and when their full import is grasped" (LW 5: 159, emphasis added).

From the viewpoint of the Köln Interactive Constructivism program, I think that it is a worthwhile challenge to further elaborate on the methodological pluralism contained in Dewey's philosophical approach with regard to the changed contexts of our own time. We should today interpret Dewey's experimentalism in its most generous cultural sense—understood as the construction, deconstruction, and continual reconstruction of a diversity of flexible methods for solving diverse and changing problems, methods that are developed in social cooperation and time and again have to be tested through application in experience.[11] To my mind, experimentalism in this broad sense still seems to be one of our most important cultural resources. It comprises scientific methods in all of their diversity as methods among others—such as artistic methods, arts of communication and arts of living, philosophical reflection, and therapeutic and educational methods. All of these methods must be seen within their own "limits of context." The constructivist criterion here is cultural viability. It implies, among other things, that we may find that in certain contexts and with regard to certain purposes some methods (e.g., scientific methods) are better fitted and yield more reliable results than other methods (e.g., creationism). There are standards of observation, experimentation, and discourse within our culture that can be defended against arbitrariness or narrow dogmatisms. But there is no overall approach to "reality." Different versions of reality call for different approaches. The potential realm of experimentalism stretches beyond any established scientific or other cultural practice. To emphasize this point helps us prevent the narrow and reductionistic (mis)understandings, which the term *scientific method* easily provokes. The more we do experimentalism in science and culture, the more diversified our methodological pluralism and our constructed results will be. Following Dewey, it is a key question for democratic societies whether they decide and are able to develop experimentalism in this broad sense. The idea of "social intelligence" that is at the heart of his talk about the "scientific method" gives us one crucial philosophical resource among others for responding to this challenge.

As to the idea of "social progress," I think that it must today be critically qualified by an ambivalence theory of social developments that reflects important aspects of (post)modern cultural analyses (see, e.g., Bauman 1993, 1997). This theory suggests that we abandon the idea of an overall and unambiguous progress and displace it with a more sober acknowledgment of the gains *and* losses implied in all social developments without trying to play off one side against the other. Given our ambivalent experiences with the political, cultural, scientific, and technological developments in the twentieth-century, I think that this interpretation is more appropriate to our (post)modern situation. There is, of course, the possibility of relative betterments of social ills in specific cases and within a limited frame of time, and in this sense democratic meliorism and reconstruction are still indispensable social ideals. But we have become skeptical as to a general line of progress projected into the horizon of (post)modern expectations. The recognition of ambivalence enhances our sense for the relativity of imaginations such as "progress" and for the diverse and contradictory contexts from which they emerge. From this perspective, one might even be tempted to interpret Dewey's criticisms of the naive progressivism held by some of his contemporaries as a first step toward the deconstruction of a modern metanarrative. And it should be noted that Dewey's "democratic experimentalism," based on intelligent methods of social problem solving and reconstruction through public inquiry and deliberation, is itself an experiment that in many respects has still to be tried out. Among others, the books of James Campbell (1992), Michael Eldridge (1998), and William R. Caspary (2000) give rich and instructive examples of how a Deweyan model of democratic experimentalism can serve today as an important critical and constructive approach.

2.2. Social Interaction and Social Control

A second and closely related line of necessary philosophical reconstruction, I suggest, concerns Dewey's ideas about "social interaction" and "social control." William J. Gavin has argued that there is an implicit tension in Dewey's philosophy between the ideas of "interacting with a context" and "trying to control and manipulate that context from outside" (2003, 70). Despite Dewey's overall interactionist approach, Gavin thinks that he was "occasionally guilty of 'control' language" of a restricted and one-sided type (ibid.). The problem with this language is that it tends to underestimate the relative indeterminacy of contexts and to succumb to a management model of regulation and domination. Gavin gives examples from *Reconstruction in Philosophy*, where Dewey uses this kind of language with regard to the management, mechanization, control, and subduing of nature (see ibid., 70f. cf. MW 12: 107, 120 ff.). But the general spirit of technological feasibility characteristic of his age also penetrates some of Dewey's thought about social reform and amelioration. He repeatedly uses rather mechanistic metaphors such as "social machinery" and "constructive social engineering" (e.g., MW 10:

241) in his discussion of the necessary means for responding to existing social needs and evils. These metaphors seem to suggest that the social reconstruction of existing practices, routines, traditions, and institutions can be technologically "mastered" in the same way that, say, a mechanic fixes a car. But, as Gavin duly observes, "Institutions . . . have been known to demonstrate their own intractability, that is, their own unwillingness to be dominated or controlled" (72). And one may suppose that Dewey's talk about "social engineering" or similar concepts was one reason for the widespread misunderstanding that he wished to install expert control as a primary means for social regulation. This clearly runs counter to his democratic ideal of public communication, negotiation, and deliberation among all of those affected by the direct or indirect consequences of transactions as the primary basis of political decision making (see LW 2: 245f.).

Moreover, we must acknowledge that today the cultural contexts with regard to ideas about social interaction and control have changed again considerably and in many ways in comparison to Dewey's lifetime. Gavin mentions our changed relation to life and death, the extended globalization of contexts (e.g., through electronic communication, nuclear power, and the worldwide market) and the growing significance of gender (75 ff.). And I may add that, speaking more generally, we have learned upon the whole to see natural, social and cultural environments in new ways that clearly point beyond early twentieth-century ideas of external regulation and control. For example, we had to learn much—and on an increasingly global scale—about the unintended consequences of our technologies, scientific applications, and social interventions. These experiences have made many of us more skeptical and cautious about our alleged powers of control. They have found expression for example, in new ecological movements or the diagnosis of a risk society in late modernity (see Beck 1986). Systems theory has taught us to understand families, organizations, schools, markets, and other social institutions as complex systems in complex contexts that resist external regulation (see, e.g., Luhmann 1988). In this changed situation, we must draw new and extended conclusions from Dewey's insistence on the philosophic necessity of taking context into account. Among other things, we must learn a new sense of technological "humility" that cautions us against the largely still predominant spirit of shortsighted feasibility. Or, as Gavin puts it, we must resist "the temptation to over manage" if we are to preserve and further elaborate a "pluralistic contextualism, that is, a fat, or thick, or diversified view of reality where, although all of the different views of the universe have meaning and some connections among them do exist, nonetheless there is no one basic conceptual connection underlying all the various interpretations. No one way to attain control is either possible or desirable" (Gavin 2003, 79).

In a word, Deweyans should today jettison older concepts of social engineering and control on behalf of a more thoroughly interactionist approach to social philosophy. They may, again, find many productive clues for this necessary reconstruction work in Dewey's own writings. His profound insights into the indispensability of "interacting with a context" provide many helpful suggestions. For example, Dewey's introduction of the term *transaction* in *Knowing and the Known* (LW 16: 1–279) can help us distinguish a more reductionist from a broader and more contextual understanding of interaction. Interaction in the contextual sense—or what Dewey calls "transaction"—means that the interacting elements are themselves constituted and constructed in the interactive process.[12] They emerge with increasing definiteness within the context of interaction. Objects, methods, and identities are seen as socially coconstructed in mutual interdependence. Accordingly, instead of trying to "will" control over contexts, we must learn to see control as something that arises from within. This contextual understanding stands in sharp contrast to more reductionist theories that assume that the interacting elements are ready-made and given in advance. It insists that "interaction" is more than a mere exchange of external input and output between fixed entities. It implies a genuinely pluralist understanding of meanings and identities that is sensitive to the multiple and changing cultural contexts of experience.

Interactive constructivism offers, among other things, three central metaperspectives for the reflection and further elaboration of a contextual understanding of social interactions (see Reich 1998a, 1998b; Neubert 2002). These perspectives, which for reasons of brevity I can only indicate here, can be helpful conceptual tools for reconstructing Dewey's philosophical pluralism today (see also Reich 2004, forthcoming).

The *first metaperspective* situates social interactions in the context of cultural practices, routines, and institutions. Humans are seen as *observers, participants, and agents.* These three roles designate different relations to context that can be distinguished, though not separated. As observers, we see, hear, sense, perceive, and interpret our world. We construct our versions of reality on the basis of our beliefs and expectations, our interests, habits, and reflections. As participants, we partake in the larger contexts of the multiple and often heterogeneous communities of interpreters that provide basic orientation in our cultural universe. We participate in social groups, communities, networks, and institutions of all kinds. Our partaking is an indispensable cultural resource, but it also implies commitments, responsibilities, loyalties, and the exclusion of certain alternatives. As agents, we act and experience. We communicate and cooperate and struggle with others. We devise plans and projects to carry out our intentions. We articulate ourselves and respond to the articulation of others.

The *second metaperspective* distinguishes between the viewpoints of *self-observers* and *distant observers.* As self-observers, we observe ourselves and others in the cultural practices in which we find ourselves immediately involved as observers, participants, and agents. We observe ourselves from within the context of our interactions with others. As distant observers, we observe others in their cultural practices and interactions in which we are not directly involved. We observe from a distance (in time or space or reflection), that is, from a different context of observation and reflection. This shift of context is of course only a gradual distinction. Transitions are fluid. As distant observers we remain self-observers within our own contexts of observation, while as self-observers we can always project ourselves into the position of an imagined distant observer and try to observe ourselves "from outside." But it is an important distinction because it helps us reflect more systematically on the contextual limits of our own interactions and prevents us from simply taking our own immediate context of observation for granted.

The *third metaperspective* concerns the level of *discourses*. Interactive constructivism distinguishes four central aspects of discourses that further help specify the multilayered cultural contexts of interactions (see Reich 1998b; Neubert and Reich 2000, 2002). Each can be seen and reflected either from a self-observer or from a distant-observer position. The first aspect is that of *power relations and hegemonies*. Discourses are part of hegemonic formations. They imply struggles for recognition and the power of interpretation. There is "no innocent discourse" (Hall 1992a, 293ff.) with regard to power. The second aspect concerns *truth claims and knowledge*. All discourses imply the production of knowledge and the determination of criteria for truth. The third aspect is that of *lived relationships*. Discourses can only take place through the interactions and communications of subjects as observers, participants, and agents. These subjects do not only construct, deconstruct, and reconstruct the contents of discourse but also their relationships as self and others within their discursive contexts. The fourth aspect concerns *the unconscious* as a limiting condition of all discourses. It reminds us that as observers, participants, and agents in discourses, we repeatedly stumble on the limits of our understanding, insight, and reflection. It stands for the unknown or not-yet known, the incomprehensible and alien within others and ourselves.

Interactive constructivism claims that, taken together, these three constructivist metaperspectives can help us better understand the complexity of heterogeneous contexts underlying the social interactions in our pluralistic cultural world. They may enhance our sense for the indispensable plurality of perspectives contained in the cultural construction of realities.

2.3. Democratic Communication and Power Relations

A third line of necessary reconstruction has already been touched by implication and should at least be rendered a bit more explicit before coming to a close. It has been mentioned that Dewey's ideal of democracy presupposes the articulation and recognition of differences as an indispensable condition of democratic communications. This raises questions about the relation between social interests in connection to power asymmetries and the development of democratic communications. That Dewey was not blind to such questions is evident, among other things, from his extensive and penetrating cultural criticism of American capitalism, especially after the experiences of the Great Depression. He repeatedly charges the existing "economic and legal institutional conditions" with erecting and petrifying barriers to democratic communication and fostering division and separation (see LW 10: 27; cf. also 14). "Life is compartmentalized and the institutionalized compartments are classified as high and as low; their values as profane and spiritual, as material and ideal. . . . Compartmentalization of occupations and interests brings about separation of that mode of activity commonly called 'practice' from insight, of imagination from executive doing, of significant purpose from work, of emotion from thought and doing" (26 ff.). Dewey makes clear in his political writings of this period that, for him, a democratic politics of recognition must be accompanied by an equally democratic politics of (re-)distribution lest the economic order increasingly become a thread to democracy (see, e.g., LW 5: 90 ff., LW 11: 41 ff.). And he also recognizes that science in the modern world does not take place outside of institutions and power relations and forcefully denounces the corruption of science on behalf of anti-democratic tendencies (see, e.g., LW 13: 156 ff., 275). These criticisms are worthwhile reading today—despite the changes of context, for example, with regard to the much more globalized economies of our time that pose new problems and require new answers (cf. Gavin 2003, 78 ff.). But Dewey did not develop a systematic critical theory of power comparable to more recent approaches to radical democracy and hegemony, for example, in the work of Ernesto Laclau and Chantal Mouffe (see Laclau 1990; Laclau and Mouffe 1991; Mouffe 1996, 2000). Seen from today's perspective, his discussion of issues of power contains certain "blind spots" that call for critical reconstruction.

Some of these weak points have recently been examined by Charlene Haddock Seigfried (2002). Drawing on her discussion,

I want to briefly mention three points here. First, Dewey often shows a tendency to (mis-)interpret conflicts of power as lack of common understanding about interests. "By locating conflicts in different approaches to life and not in struggles for power, he frequently underestimates what is required to overcome them. He seems to think that once someone has participated in a rational process of inquiry, she or he would not persist in holding onto prejudices or unilateral power." Therefore "his analyses often do not go far enough" (55 ff.). To my mind, Dewey's holistic vision of democracy as the "Great Community" (see LW 2: 325 ff.) forms part of the background of this shortcoming (see Neubert 2004a, 2004b, forthcoming). Second, focusing his cultural criticism on economic inequalities and oppression, Dewey often tends to underestimate processes of discrimination and marginalization, for example, due to racism (see also Sullivan 2003; Haddock Seigfried in this book) and gender prejudice (see Garrison and Haddock Seigfried in this book).[13] Seen from today's perspective, political developments and social movements—such as feminism, civil rights, and other minority movements—have sharpened our awareness in the twentieth-century of the complexities of power relations in late-capitalist societies. For example, the complex intersections of classism, racism, and sexism (e.g., misogyny and homophobia) as relatively independent lines of power that cannot be simply reduced to one another have become the theme of many critical analyses of contemporary multicultural societies (see, e.g., Bradley 1992). Third, Dewey upon the whole "fails to follow through with an account of the role that power plays in human affairs." Especially, he does not sufficiently explore "in detail how it alters the lives of those affected by it" (Haddock Seigfried 2002, 55), that is, the consequences of power asymmetries in the experiences of those who are discriminated against or marginalized. And I may add that the relevance of this objection for the reconstruction of pragmatist social thought is underlined, to my mind, by the observation that it equally applies to present-day neo-pragmatists such as Richard Rorty (cf., e.g., Rorty 1999).

These criticisms pose important challenges for the work of reconstructing pragmatic social philosophy. "The end of democracy is a radical end" writes Dewey in *Democracy Is*

Radical, "for it is an end that has not been adequately realized in any country at any time" (LW 11: 298 f.; emphasis in original). It requires great changes in existing economic, legal, and cultural institutions. And it is a vision whose meanings and implications time and again must be explored and negotiated anew. Reconstructing Dewey's philosophical pluralism, we should today make use of the most up-to-date theoretical resources of our time to rethink the idea of radical democracy in the frame of our own societal and cultural contexts. From the perspective of interactive constructivism, I think that this requires a number of theoretical "border crossings." Many approaches in contemporary cultural research bear productive affinities for pragmatist and constructivist social thought. But some of these approaches have been developed in discursive circles and traditions with which pragmatists and constructivists so far have not sufficiently come into contact and exchange. I am thinking, for example, of work done in fields such as cultural studies, gender studies, and postcolonial studies (see Neubert 2002, 2004a, forthcoming; Hall 1992a, 1996; Hall and DuGay 1996). To my mind, many of the researches and theoretical perspectives developed in these fields are highly suggestive for the project of rethinking radical democracy in the face of the multicultural societies of our increasingly globalized world. To elaborate on these theoretical intersections and their implications seems to me a promising task for both pragmatists and constructivists.

Notes

1. Several other chapters in this book deal with pluralist philosophical implications in Deweyan pragmatism and throw additional light on what is said here. For example, Green explores questions of diversity and difference in the contemporary application of pragmatism's political philosophy and theory of democracy. Similarly, Haddock Seigfried's chapter elaborates on differences in the context of philosophical perspectivism. Garrison explains why pragmatism's emphasis on pluralism and the recognition of differences are important for a contemporary (gender sensitive) ethics of communication. Finally, see Reich's constructivist interpretation of diversity and difference in the context of democratic education.

2. For an introduction, see Reich (2002). Theoretical foundations are extensively discussed in Reich (1998a,1998b). For connections to Dewey's pragmatism, see Neubert (1998) and Hickman, Neubert, and Reich (2004, forthcoming). A short English introduction to the Köln program is given by Neubert (2003).

3. Although he warns us that "what is called 'modern' is as yet unformed" and "inchoate" (MW 12: 273), this development, in his view, has greatly been advanced by the "scientific," the "industrial," and the "political revolution" of modernity (257).

4. Earlier in this book Reich explored the relevance of Dewey's pragmatist theory of habit for a democratic theory of educational growth. For a further discussion of Dewey's understanding of experience, habit, and growth, see Garrison's chapter later in this book.

5. With regard to the complex relationship of feelings, desires, attitudes, selective interests, and reflection in Deweyan social philosophy and criticism, see Haddock Seigfried's chapter in this book, where she gives many instructive examples (e.g., from the history of pragmatist feminism).

6. To my mind, this is especially true for present-day constructivist approaches that can find many connections to and affinities for his pragmatic and constructive philosophy (see Hickman, Neubert, and Reich 2004).

7. Boisvert criticizes Dewey as a philosopher with a "fresh start view of time" (2003, 90) that sometimes leads to simplifications and exaggerated claims. His criticism is partly suggestive, even if one does not share Boisvert's overall metaphysical project and the conservative turn of his argument.

8. For a critical reading, see Sullivan (2003).

9. With regard to Dewey's concept of scientific method and his theory of social inquiry, see also Hans Seigfried's contribution in this book.

10. In the 1948 new introduction to "Reconstruction in Philosophy," Dewey approvingly quotes C. D. Darlington: "Scientific discovery is often carelessly looked upon as the creation of some new knowledge which can be added to the great body of old knowledge. This is true of the strictly trivial discoveries. It is not true of the fundamental discoveries, such as those of the laws of mechanics, of chemical combination, of evolution, on which scientific advance ultimately

depends. These always entail the destruction of or disintegration of old knowledge *before the new can be created....* We need a Ministry of Disturbance, a regulated source of annoyance; a destroyer of routine; an underminer of complacency" (MW 12: 262 ff., emphasis in original).

11. Interactive constructivism uses the three terms *construction*, *deconstruction*, and *reconstruction* as closely related perspectives that mutually complement each other (see Reich 2002, Neubert and Reich 2002; Neubert 2003).

12. Dewey coauthored this book with Arthur F. Bentley. It was one of his last philosophical writings.

13. Garrison's elaboration on issues of emotional dismissal in his chapter in this book is a good example of how the underestimation of power in Dewey's philosophy of communication can be retheorized and partially overcome from within a pragmatist social perspective.

Works Cited

Bauman, Z. 1993. *Modernity and ambivalence.* Cambridge: Polity.
————. 1997. *Postmodernity and its discontents.* Cambridge: Polity Press.
Beck, U. 1986. *Risikogesellschaft.* Frankfurt a. M.: Suhrkamp.
Boisvert, R. D. 1992. Metaphysics as the search for paradigmatic instances. *Transactions of the Charles S. Peirce Society* 28.2: 189–202.
————. 2003. As Dewey was Hegelian, so we should be Deweyan. In *Dewey's wake: Unfinished work of pragmatic reconstruction,* ed. W. Gavin, 89–108. Albany: State University of New York Press.
Bradley, H. 1992. Changing social divisions: Class, gender and race. In *Social and cultural forms of modernity,* ed. R. Bocock and K. Thompson, 11–67. Cambridge: Polity Press.
Campbell, J. 1992. *The community reconstructs: The meaning of pragmatic social thought.* Urbana: University of Illinois Press.
Caspary R. 2000. *Dewey on democracy.* Ithaca, NY, and London: Cornell University Press.
Dykhuizen, G. 1973. *The life and mind of John Dewey.* Carbondale: Southern Illinois University Press.

Eldridge, M. 1998. *Transforming experience: John Dewey's cultural instrumentalism*. Nashville, TN, and London: Vanderbilt University Press.

Gavin, W. J. 2003. Contexts vibrant and contexts souring. In *In Dewey's wake: Unfinished work of pragmatic reconstruction*, ed. W. Gavin, 63–85. Albany: State University of New York Press.

Hall, S. 1992a. The question of cultural identity. In *Modernity and its futures*, eds. S. Hall, D. Held, and T. McGrew, 273–316. Cambridge: Polity Press.

———. 1992b. The West and the rest—Discourse and power. In *Formations of modernity*, ed. S. Hall and B. Gieben, 275–310. Cambridge: Polity Press.

———. 1996. When was "the post-colonial"? Thinking at the limit. In *The Post-Colonial question: common skies, divided horizons*, ed. L. Chambers and L. Curti, 242–260. London: Routledge.

———. 1997. Ed. *Representation: Cultural representations and signifying practices*. London: Sage Publications and the Open University.

Hall, S., and P. DuGay. 1996. *Questions of cultural identity*. London, Thousand Oaks, CA, and New Delhi: Sage Publications.

Hickman, L., S. Neubert, and K. Reich. Eds. 2004. *John Dewey: Zwischen Pragmatismus und Konstruktivismus Reihe: Interaktionistischer Konstruktivismus*, Bd. 1 Münster u.a.: Waxmann.

———. Forthcoming. *John Dewey—Between pragmatism and constructivism*.

James, W. 1958. *Talks to teachers on psychology and to students on some of life's ideals*. New York: Holt.

Laclau, E. 1990. *New reflections on the revolution of our time*. London and New York: Verso.

Laclau, E., and C. Mouffe. 1991. *Hegemonie und radikale Demokratie: Zur Dekonstruktion des Marxismus*. Wien: Passagen.

Luhmann, N. 1988. *Soziale Systeme*. Frankfurt a. M.: Suhrkamp.

Mouffe, C. 1996. *Deconstruction and pragmatism*. New York: Routledge.

———. 2000. *The Democratic paradox*. London: Verso.

Neubert, S. 1998. Erkenntinis, Verhalten und Kommunikation: John Deweys Philosophie des "experience" in interak-

tionistisch-konstruktivistischer Interpretation. Münster u.a.:
Waxmann.
————. 2002. Konstruktivismus, Demokratie und Multikultur.
In *Multikulturalität in der Diskussion. Neuere Beiträge zu
einem umstrittenen Konzept*, ed. S. Neubert, H. J. Roth, and
E. Yildiz, 63-98. Opladen: Leske Budrich.
————. 2003. Some perspectives of interactive constructivism
on the theory of education. University of Cologne.
Retrieved April 22, 2007 (see "Texte": "Introduction").
http://www.konstruktivismus.uni-koeln.de.
————. 2004a. Eine neue (Allgemein-) Bildung?: Herausford-
erungen durch die, cultural studies Tertium Compara-
tionis. *Journal für International und Interkulturell
Vergleichende Erziehungswissenschaft* 10:1, 82–104. Münster,
New York, München, Berlin: Waxmann.
————. 2004b. Pragmatismus, Konstruktivismus und
Kulturtheorie. In *John Dewey: Zwischen Pragmatismus und
Konstruktivismus*, L. Hickman, S. Neubert, and K. Reich,
ed. Bd.1. Münster, New York, München, Berlin: Wax-
man,114–131.
————. Forthcoming. pragmatism, constructivism, and the
theory of culture." In *John Dewey—Between pragmatism and
constructivism*, ed. L. Hickman, S. Neubert, and K. Reich.
Neubert, S., and K. Reich. 2000. Die konstruktivistische
Erweiterung der Diskustheorie: Eine Einführung in die
interaktionistisch-konstruktive Sicht von Diskursen. In *Die
Idee des Diskurses: Interdisziplinäre Annäherungen*, ed. H.
Burckhart, H. Gronke, and J. P. Brune, 43–74. Markt
Schwaben: Eusl.
————. 2002. Toward a constructivist theory of discourse.
Retrieved April 22, 2007 (see "Texte": "English").
http://www.konstruktivismus.uni-koeln.de.
Reich, K. 1998a. *Die Ordnung der Blicke: Perspektiven des interak-
tionistischen Konstruktivismus Band 1: Beobachtung und die
Unschärfen der Erkenntnis*. Neuwied u.a.: Luchterhand.
————. 1998b. *Die Ordnung der Blicke: Perspektiven des interak-
tionistischen Konstruktivismus. Band 2: Beziehungen und
Lebenswelt*. Neuwied u.a.: Luchterhand.

————. 2002. *Systemisch-konstruktivistische Pädagogik: Einführung in Grundlagen einer interaktionistisch-konstruktivistischen Pädagogik*. Neuwied u.a.: Luchterhand.

————. 2004. Beobachter, Teilnehmer und Akteure in Diskursen—zur Bobachtertheorie *in Pragmatismus und Konstruktivismus*. In *John Dewey: Zwischen Pragmatismus und Konstruktivismus Reihe: Interaktionistischer Konstruktivismus*. Bd. 1 ed. L. Hickman, S. Neubert, K. Reich, 76–98. Bd. 1. Münster, New York, München, Berlin: Waxmann.

————. Forthcoming. Observers, participants, and agents in discourses—A consideration of pragmatist and constructivist theories of the observer. In *John Dewey—Between pragmatism and constructivism*, ed. L. Hickman, S. Neubert, and K. Reich. New York, N.Y.: Fordham University Press.

Rorty, R. 1999. *Achieving our country*. Cambridge, MA, and London: Harvard University Press.

Seigfried, C. H. 2002. John Dewey's pragmatist feminism. In *Feminist interpretations of John Dewey*, ed. C. H. Seigfried, 47-77. University Park: Pennsylvania State University Press.

Sullivan, S. 2003. (Re)construction zone: Beware of falling statues. In *In Dewey's wake: Unfinished work of pragmatic reconstruction*, ed. W. Gavin, 109–27. Albany: State University of New York Press.

Westbrook, R. B. 1991. *John Dewey and American democracy*. Ithaca, NY, and London: Cornell University Press.

Chapter 5

Evolutionary Naturalism, Logic, and Lifelong Learning: Three Keys to Dewey's Philosophy of Education

Larry A. Hickman

Anyone who follows accounts of public discourse in the United States is surely aware that there is a determined resurgence of demands on the part of religionists in certain quarters, including highly placed members of government, that their anti-scientific (non-naturalist) views of the origin of human life be taught in the public schools. Whereas it seemed apparent to some observers that such battles were finished in the 1920s, when the judgment in the famous Scopes trial in Dayton, Tennessee, was handed down, it has now become evident that there is among the citizenry of the United States a serious backlash against what is best called a scientific worldview that incorporates varieties of naturalism that may be called "cosmological," "methodological," and "ethical."

As a part of their rejection of cosmological naturalism, an alarmingly high percentage of Americans confess their belief in a six-day creation of the world during which the first human

beings also were created in their present form. As evidence of
this, I cite a CBS News poll from November 22, 2004. Fifty-
five percent of those polled believe that God created humans
in their present form. Twenty-seven percent believe that
humans have evolved, but that God guided the process. Only
13 percent believe that humans have evolved, and that God
did not guide the process. Translated into the arena of decisions about secondary school curriculum, some 65 percent of
all Americans would like to see creationism taught alongside
evolution. Perhaps even more alarmingly, 37 percent of all
Americans want creationism taught *instead* of evolution.
Among those who voted for George W. Bush, that number
rises to 45 percent.

Even some well-respected academics appear to have joined
this backlash against science (or at least against science as it
has been conducted for the last 350 years). Notre Dame
University philosopher Alvin Plantinga, for example, has
called for an "Augustinian science," which, he argues, would
involve pursuing science "using all that we know: what we
know about God as well as what we know about his creation,
and what we know by faith as well as what we know in other
ways." Plantinga (1998) rejects what he calls "the Grand
Evolutionary Myth," along with what he calls "Methodological Naturalism," or the view that "for any study of the
world to qualify as 'scientific' it cannot refer to God's creative
activity (or any sort of divine activity)"

For his part, President Bush has registered his opinion that
"On the issue of evolution, the verdict is still out on how God
created the Earth" (Duff 2002). Perhaps even more ominously,
he has either dismissed or sought to suppress scientific studies
of the effects of global warming and other pressing problems.[1]
These positions would be bad enough were they just isolated
incidents. They have in fact become part of a much broader
assault on the results of scientific investigation, and therefore
the methods and outlooks of science that have been developed
painstakingly and with great cost since the seventeenth century.
In his contribution to this book, James Campbell reminds us
that Dewey defined government through its "adaptive func-

tion." It is difficult to imagine how a government that seeks to suppress the results of scientific studies can provide much in the way of "adaptive function."

In the case of Professor Plantinga, we appear to have a case of attempted invasion by supernaturalism of the variety of scientific naturalism that has been developed over the last 350 years. In the far more dangerous case of Mr. Bush, it appears that a mixture of supernaturalism, political ideology, and electoral expediency is trumping what I am calling "evolutionary naturalism."

It is not my purpose in this chapter to proceed further into a discussion of what is faulty, and even dangerous, in the positions taken by Professor Plantinga and Mr. Bush (although I reserve the right to treat both positions tangentially). In my view, Michael Ruse has already accomplished that task quite well in the case of Professor Plantinga (Ruse 2001, especially 58–65, 100–11). As for Mr. Bush and his science policy, as I write, more than 5,000 scientists, including 48 Nobel laureates, 62 National Medal of Science recipients, and 127 members of the National Academy of Sciences, have signed a document that characterizes the current administration's policies as being in conflict with sound scientific theory and practice.[2]

Instead, I intend to use such anti-naturalist positions as foils for a discussion of what I take to be an acceptable form of naturalism, which is linked via a well-crafted theory of inquiry to a robust educational philosophy that includes a commitment to programs of lifelong learning. All of this I find in the work of John Dewey, and especially in his work as it pertains to fostering the goals and ideals of life in pluralistic democracies.

What Is Different about Dewey's Version of Naturalism?

Joseph Margolis has argued that the naturalism of the founding pragmatists, including Dewey, is very different from the naturalism of W. V. O. Quine, Donald Davidson, and Richard Rorty. In fact, writing of the transformation from the earlier to the later form of naturalism, Margolis claims that there is a movement that is "absolutely fundamental to the history and

future of American philosophy," and that, moreover, the "naturalizing" of Quine and Davidson "is demonstrably incompatible
with the pragmatism of the classic figures" (2002, 6).

What is this difference? For the original pragmatists,
Margolis writes, "Naturalism is little more than a refusal to
admit non-natural or supernatural resources in the descriptive
or explanatory discourse of any truth-bearing kind." In contrast,
"naturalizers" Quine and Davidson have held that: "(1) truth-
bearing is ultimately causal; (2) causal explanation is constrained
by the 'causal closure of the physical'; (3) all description, analysis, and explanation of mental and cultural phenomena are para-
phrasable in accord with doctrines (1) and (2) if admissible at
all, or else they conform with some version of supervenientism; . . . and (4) pertinent inquiries, claims, and explanations
that fail to meet the conditions of doctrines (1)–(3)—notably,
epistemological 'explanations'—are senseless or philosophically
illegitimate" (2002, 6–7). Margolis's argument, in brief, is that
the founding pragmatists, including Dewey, argued that the real
world is natural but not naturalizable, and that this distinction is
the key to the future success of the positions constructed by the
classical pragmatists.

As Margolis characterizes the situation, then, naturalizers
such as Quine and Davidson have erred in the sense that they
have impoverished the broad reach of naturalism as it is
encountered in the works of the founding pragmatists. They
have supplanted a broadly intuitive cosmological naturalism
with a narrowly constructed account of physical causality. Their
variety of naturalism, without more, cannot therefore take into
account a broad range of human, which is to say natural, activities such as those that are characterized in "spiritual" terms.
They therefore appear to have missed the point made so forcefully by William James and John Dewey, for example, that
human spirituality is natural because it is human behavior, and
humans are natural organisms. This, of course, is not to dismiss
the pertinent observation of Judith Green, in her contribution
to this book, that religion can be one of the most divisive elements in the body politic. My point instead is to insist, with
Campbell, in his chapter, that since human religious impulses
and feelings are part of nature, then qua natural they are open

to the possibility of reconstruction along lines that might eventually produce a "common faith."

More specifically, what are the elements of the "naturalism without naturalizing" that one finds in the work of Dewey? First, there is the notion that there is *no need* to go outside of the realm of human experience to allegedly transcendent or supernatural sources in order to understand or account for what is difficult, problematic, or even sublime or "spiritual" within human experience. Furthermore, *if one does* attempt to go outside the natural world of human experience to what is transcendent or supernatural in order to secure norms, standards, and absolutes, then appeals to authority, a priorism, or the dead weight of tradition are sure to follow.

Second, unlike the program of the naturalizers, Dewey's version of naturalism does not entail reductionism of the materialistic or physicalist variety, or for that matter any other variety of reductionism.[3] This idea is securely nested within the pluralism of what William James called "radical empiricism," and what Dewey called "the postulate of immediate empiricism." On this view, body and mind, matter and "spirit," as well as form and matter are not prior to our experience of the world but consequent on inquiry into and reconstruction of it. The dualities just mentioned thus become functional distinctions, not ontological ones that may or may not be of help in situations where inquiry is called for. Dewey's position thus obviates the problems associated with the supervenientism of the naturalizers. It dissolves the issue by de-ontologizing, that is, functionalizing and instrumentalizing, the underlying duality.

Third, Dewey's version of naturalism is a cosmological position that is opposed to supernaturalism in the sense that there is closure within the space-time-causal system that is studied by science. But it is not the reductive theory of causality proposed by the naturalizers. Dewey offered instead a very spare notion of causality linked to an instrumental definition of "cause," namely, "its service in giving control of future experience" (MW 6: 381). For Dewey, a cause is an element or factor within a total problematic situation that has been isolated from other elements or factors as a result of inquiry and has been determined to afford the opportunity, when altered in appropriate ways, to allow greater control over the problematic situation.

It might be objected that this position ignores the fact that there are causes of events over which we cannot in fact exercise greater control. One example of this would appear to be inquiry into the cause(s) of the extinction of the dinosaurs. As we know, paleontologists, astronomers, climatologists, and others are working on this issue. Some of these scientists claim to have isolated a "cause" or "causes" of the event—not in the sense that they can control a future occurrence of a similar event, but that they can instead control the future occurrence of doubts or uncertainties with respect to their scientific accounts. Moreover, the repeatability of an experiment should not be confused with the repeatability of an event, which is the subject of the experiment; otherwise paleontology would be impossible. Alvin Plantinga (1998), for example, appears to make this simple error when he confuses the big bang theory qua an *unrepeatable event* with experiments that have led to its *hypothesis*.

Fourth, and perhaps most importantly, it follows from the fact that Dewey's version of naturalism is pluralistic, instead of reductionistic, that it leaves open a "way by which we can be genuinely naturalistic and yet maintain cherished values, provided they are critically clarified and reinforced" (LW 1: 4). As Hans Seigfried eloquently argues in his contribution to this book, Dewey's naturalism is thus far removed from the odiously reductive positivism with which he has been so often charged. "An empirical method which remains true to nature," he writes, "does not 'save'; it is not an insurance device nor a mechanical antiseptic. But it inspires the mind with courage and vitality to create new ideals and values in the face of the perplexities of a new world" (4). In short, and contrary to Dewey's critics, his naturalism does not simply destroy values—it analyses and reconstructs them in ways that can contribute to the maintenance and growth of the types of outlooks and institutions that are required if pluralistic democracies are to flourish. Taken together, these features of Dewey's thought provide a firm basis for democratic institutions that are both pluralistic and vigorous in the sense of self-correcting.

A Naturalistic Theory of Inquiry

In his 1938 *Logic: The Theory of Inquiry* (LW 12), Dewey connected his naturalism to his theory of inquiry. "The naturalistic conception of logic, which underlies the position here taken," he wrote, "is thus cultural naturalism. Neither inquiry nor the most abstractly formal set of symbols can escape from the cultural matrix in which they live, move and have their being" (28).

What this means in practice is that his theory of inquiry rejects a priorisms in general; it treats metaphysical, epistemological, and theological presuppositions not as foundations to be shoved *under* inquiry, as it were, but as hypotheses to be examined *by* inquiry in order to determine whether they are warranted and assertible.[4] It also rejects other types of "foundations," such as those that are putatively psychological and offered under the names of sense-data, mental faculties, and so on. Inquiry is thus for Dewey naturalistic in the sense that it arises out of a cultural matrix and returns to that cultural matrix in order to do its work. Another way of putting this is that Dewey not only rejected versions of knowledge getting that depend on what is supernatural, but also those that depend on what is extranatural as well— including putative sources, such as intuition or some higher faculty of reason, which are merely stipulated.

Dewey's treatment of inquiry highlights the "evolutionary" part of his evolutionary naturalism and forms an easy transition into his ideas about lifelong learning. His naturalism is evolutionary in at least two important senses. First, it seeks to do for philosophical inquiry what Darwin did for biology, that is, to undercut the notion that values, concepts, and abstract entities are fixed and finished in the same sense in which biological species were once thought to have been fixed through special creation and therefore cut off from the possibility of future development. This was the burden of Dewey's well-known essay "The Influence of Darwin on Philosophy," published in 1909 (MW 4: 3–13).

Second, Dewey's naturalism is evolutionary in the sense that "it is concerned with the manner or process by which anything comes into experienced existence" (MW 2: 5). Dewey utilized several different terms to identify this method of inquiry. He identified it as the "evolutionary method," the "genetic method," and the "experimental method" (5). Regardless of terminology, however, his point is clear: "[S]tatements arrived at by experimental science are of an historical order. They take their rise in, and they find their application to, a world of unique and changing things: an evolutionary universe" (8).

These two aspects of his evolutionary naturalism have interesting consequences for inquiry into moral values, which is of course central to Dewey's philosophy of education. It is clear enough that his position allows him to reject various forms of supernaturalism and extranaturalism such as the ones I have already mentioned, for example, intuitionism. Of course, he does not dispute the fact that we have intuitions. But intuitions are treated as raw materials for *judgments* about values, not as the *valuations themselves*. In order for there to be a valuation, facts must be related and put in order—they must be processed. The problem with intuitionism, in sum, is that it does not place its facts into the evolutionary or genetic relationship that provides the basis for a judgment of the objective validity of the moral claim (MW 2: 25). As Seigfried points out in her chapter in this book, ideas, including intuitions, must be "examined for their functional fitness for resolving existential conflict situations, and thus...become operational in that they instigate and direct further operations of observation."

Perhaps even more importantly, however, it also allows him to reject putatively scientific attempts to base moral theory on a model of inductive generalization, that is, one that involves the collection of data relating to moral values and practices across human populations and the abstraction from such data of common elements that are then treated as fixed. His alternative to this, his historical or evolutionary method, emphasizes the process by which what is morally valued is analyzed in concrete, emerging contexts and determined to be morally valuable within those contexts.

Even if we could find some invariant practice regarding conjugal fidelity, for example, we would still not have gained any insight into the scientific significance of that practice. Dewey identifies such scientific significance with the possibility of control of future experience, and he argues that it is disclosed

only through knowledge of historical facts and their permutation through time, that is, their evolutionary development. As
he puts the matter, "[T]he essence of moral struggle and of
moral progress lies...precisely in that region where sections of
society, or groups of individuals, are becoming conscious of the
necessity of ideals of a higher and more generalized order than
those recognized in the past. To fix upon that which has been
believed everywhere, and at all times, 'as the essential content of
the moral law,' would give practical morality a tremendous setback" (MW 2: 19). In sum, it is a central feature of Dewey's
evolutionary theory of inquiry that the scientific method concerns itself with "the discovery of a common and continuous
process, and that this can be determined only historically" (17).

There has been persistent misunderstanding of Dewey's
position on these matters. There has, for example, been a tendency on the part of some of Dewey's opponents to charge him
with extreme forms of positivism or scientism. Here, for example, is a statement of one of Dewey's harshest critics, Mortimer
Adler. Writing about what he called a "Deweyized" public
school system, Adler said: "I use the name of Dewey to symbol-
ize what Lewis Mumford describes as pragmatic liberalism—a
liberalism 'so completely deflated and debunked' that it forsakes
all the 'essential principles of ideal liberalism: justice, freedom,
truth' and hence disavows a rationally articulated moral philosophy; supposing instead that 'science,' which confessedly
despises norms, would eventually apply all the guidance necessary for human conduct" (16–17). The charge, in fine, is that
Dewey and his fellow pragmatists went over to the dark side of
the fact-value split.

I hope that it has become apparent from the preceding para-
graphs, however, that Dewey denied the very fact-value split on
which this criticism is based. Seen from the standpoint of his
evolutionary or genetic method, nested as it is in his evolutionary naturalism, facts are always facts of a case and are selected on
the basis of interests, involving values. Moreover, whereas it is a
fact that particular values are held, and perhaps even cherished,
by particular individuals, groups, and societies, it also is the case
that unless those cherished values are continually evaluated in
ways that reflect the methods of good experimental science, they

become inflexible and unsuitable for application in emerging situations. Dewey's position on this matter is precisely and concisely characterized by Jim Garrison in his chapter in this book: With an implicit reference to Dewey's 1896 "Reflex Arc" essay, he writes that "In Dewey's theory, cognition and affect are phases or subfunctions within a single functional coordination. Affect and cognition emerge and clarify themselves as phases within the larger durational-extensional process of the individual body-mind's efforts to functionally coordinate its behavior."

I find it hard to believe that any unprejudiced and candid person who has followed the presentation thus far, which has included passages in Dewey's own words, could possibly be tempted to accept the judgment of Adler and Mumford, that Dewey's pragmatism "forsakes all the 'essential principles of ideal liberalism: justice, freedom, truth' and hence disavows a rationally articulated moral philosophy Mumford cited in Adler, 1940, 16–17." Dewey is simply not guilty of the charges of extreme positivism or scientism. Regarding Dewey's alleged "scientism" it should be recalled, as Stefan Neubert pointedly does in his chapter in this book, that Dewey's understanding of experience "is much more comprehensive than any system of cognition or interpretation." And as Haddock Seigfried reminds us in her chapter, also in this book, Dewey's view of experience is radical in the sense that "it recognizes the claims and traits, of all qualitative modes and organizations of experience, instead of setting up some one form as ultimate and 'real.'"

"Genuine" or "Logical" Concepts and the Educational Process

Perhaps I can clarify the importance of Dewey's naturalism for his theory of inquiry and his philosophy of education by providing a more detailed account of what he means by a "genuine" or "logical" concept, as opposed to one that is false, misleading, or flaccid. Dewey defines the logical concept as a "factor or status in a reflective situation; it is always a predicate of judgment, in use in interpreting and developing the logical subject, or datum of perception" (MW 2: 360).

What this means in educational practice is that concepts must be constructed as a part of the learning process, not just given ready-made from some external source. As constructed, they constitute a system of attributes that has to be held together by some *determining principle*. Viewed from the inside, the principle must *control its own instances* in order to ensure that they maintain a well-integrated whole. Viewed from the outside, the principle *specifies its own limits* in such a way that it excludes everything else (MW 2: 345). The implications for educational philosophy of this admittedly technical definition are considerable. For one thing, a nominal abstraction is simply not an adequate substitute for a scientific concept. It is certainly true that the concept "color," for example, may be nominally abstracted from several variously colored blocks. This may be an appropriate way to teach a child how to use a name—in this case, the generic word "color."

But genuine or robust learning involves much more than getting control of the usage of nominal abstractions. It involves a scientific understanding of situations—in this case, an understanding of a concept—color—that goes well beyond simple taxonomic exercises. Dewey tells us that in order to construct a scientific concept of color, there must be a shift from the empirical exercise that I have just described to one that is experimental in the sense of instrumental. If we want a scientific concept of color, for example, then it must be constructed as the result of discovery and analysis of light waves, whose various frequencies constitute the various colors of the spectrum (345). It is in this way that a jumble of unordered color experiences, red, blue, and yellow blocks in a box or on a table, for example, will become parts of a color system. And this *genuine* or *logical* concept is a *scientific* concept in the sense that it can in turn serve as a tool for further investigation.

A genuine scientific concept is never completely fixed or finished. It is dynamic. It is a well-ordered arrangement of previously unordered data in what Dewey calls "a dynamic continuity of existence" (345). In other words, our use of concepts must incorporate a strong sense of fallibilism, that is, a profound appreciation for the manner in which changing circumstances and new data can undermine some of our most tightly held beliefs.

If inductive generalization is not adequate to the formation of a scientific concept of color, neither is it adequate to the formation of moral concepts. This is a particularly important point, given the charges of positivism, scientism, and even moral nihilism that continue to be leveled against Dewey's educational theories. The collection of data relating to moral values and practices across human populations and abstraction from such data of common elements that are then treated as "universal" in the sense of "fixed" does not, in Dewey's view, constitute a scientifically useful concept in the field of morals.

Scientific concepts, and therefore concepts that *activate* and are *active in* the process of learning, must be more than abstractions from enumerated data, they must have historical or genetic depth. Their formation must involve a process by which what is morally *valued* is analyzed in concrete, emerging contexts and determined to be morally *valuable* within and across those contexts. As we know, this view has put Dewey at odds with those who view education as simply the "transmission of knowledge and values."

Dewey's view that genuine concepts are plastic (but not arbitrary) is easily applicable to many current debates about moral values. One such debate that is a matter of intense concern (and legal and political dispute) in the United States as I write, and that serves as an excellent example of his view of the generation of scientific concepts in the context of moral debates, involves adoption of children by same-sex couples. According to the 2000 census, there are 250,000 children in the United States being raised by same-sex parents (Savage 2005, A27). Arguments against such arrangements are most often based either on religious authority or on inductive generalizations of the type I have just discussed.

In the former case, religious-based concepts of the nuclear family tend to be both attenuated and ossified—they take as its *determining principle* cultural practices that are most often antique and inflexible with respect to the demands of changed and changing circumstances. In the latter case, inductive generalization usually becomes circular and thus impotent, since the determining principle is selected in a manner that ensures that only cases of "correctly defined" (read "narrowly selected") families are selected as instances of the generic concept. Even if we were able to find within such narrowly selected human populations some invariant practice regarding children in same-sex households, however, we would still not have gained any insight into the *scientific significance* of that practice.

The problem is that in both cases there is a failure of scientific concept formation. In one case, good science is most often trumped by adherence to religious authority, and in the other what we have is not so much good science but faulty application of information gained through sampling. First, there is a failure to properly *identify* instances of what constitutes a successful, nurturing family situation, because the choice of the determining principle has been artificially restricted. Beyond that, however, there is a failure to *supplement* those narrowly selected instances of successful traditional family arrangements with nontraditional arrangements of the *same kind*, that is, with nontraditional familial arrangements in which children are loved and nurtured in ways that promote their healthy maturation. Finally, there is failure to *locate* instances of successful family relationships of both types—traditional and nontraditional alike—within a wider conceptual system, such as a system of laws. In his chapter in this book, Campbell provides two additional examples of current failure to acknowledge that concepts are plastic (but not arbitrary)—the distribution of medical care and teenage pregnancy.

Scientific significance is thus not based on the authority of sacred scriptures or other received traditions, nor is it a result of inductive generalization. It is instead grounded in a thoroughgoing naturalism, related to the possibility of control of future experience. Dewey argued that scientific significance, and therefore the possibility of control of future experience and the possibility of learning, is disclosed only through knowledge of historical facts and their permutation through time, that is, their evolutionary development. In the example under discussion, this would require both a careful assessment of successful child-rearing by same-sex couples, a comparison of that data with similar data derived from analyses of child-rearing by traditional heterosexual couples, and analyses of collateral issues such as those that are economic and legal. The result would be the formation of a "genuine" concept of the nuclear family that could serve as the basis for further experimentation that would be likely, in turn, to serve as the basis for legal and economic reforms. A "genuine" concept of the nuclear family is thus able to contribute to the possibility of successful control of future experience in ways that other types of concepts cannot.

As I have already indicated, Dewey thought that "[t]he essence of moral struggle and of moral progress lies... precisely in that region where sections of society, or groups of individuals, are becoming conscious of the necessity of ideals of a higher and more generalized order than those recognized in the past. To fix upon that which has been believed everywhere, and at all times, 'as the essential content of the moral law,' would give practical morality a tremendous setback" (MW 2: 19).

This is not to say that concepts do not help *standardize* our knowledge, for they do. They are instruments that anchor our thinking in a constantly changing world. As I have already suggested, they aid in the *identification* of objects and events, their *supplementation* with objects and events of the same kind, and their *location or placement* within a wider system of objects and events.

In Dewey's view, the transmission of standardized knowledge, although for the most part easily and efficiently accomplished, simply does not contribute much to robust educational practice. It leaves most pupils instead with concepts that tend to be only nominal and remote from their own experience. For learning to occur, there must be a *generalization* and *extension* of learned concepts. What Dewey calls a "genuine" or "logical" or "scientific" concept thus becomes "a working tool of further apprehensions, an instrument of understanding other things" (LW 8: 242). Dewey's theory of inquiry thus provides the means of adjudicating conflicts between and among received values—means that are necessary for pluralistic democracies. As I understand Kersten Reich's proposal for a "third criterion" in his chapter in this book, he and Dewey are of the same mind: "In a self-reflexive effort all learners must learn to see themselves—as globally as possible—as observers of their own participation in communities, and of other participations of other humans in other communities."

Lifelong Learning

If my argument up to this point has been successful, then perhaps you will agree that Dewey's evolutionary naturalism, his theory of inquiry, and his characterization of the role of genuine scientific concepts in the process of learning are key components of his philosophy of education. I have identified some trends in the public life of the United States that are undermining confidence in scientific methods and therefore the manner in which science is taught and learned. The alternative that I have offered is renewed commitment to a naturalism of the type that Dewey advanced. This would be a naturalism that would avoid the dead ends of supernaturalism and inductive abstraction as a means of concept formation as it impacts public policy in general, and especially public policy as it concerns education; it also would avoid the overly restrictive tendencies of those philosophers who have been called "naturalizers." Perhaps even more important, however, increased commitment to what Dewey calls "genuine" concept formation would arm learners with methods of inquiry that could continue to be applied and improved throughout a lifetime—long after completion of a "formal" educational process. Lifelong learning, in Dewey's view, is a key element of self-sustaining democracies.

I also have provided some concrete examples of the manner in which Dewey's treatment of genuine or scientific concept formation is applicable within the sphere of values. This is particularly important, given the fact that he continues to be charged with scientism and nihilism, that is, with being a destroyer of values. Dewey's philosophy of education was neither scientistic nor nihilistic. He did not seek to destroy values, but he did think that it is the duty of every member of a democratic society to seek ways of refining and reconstructing values in response to changing circumstances. He was not opposed to religion, but he did think that religious beliefs and associations should be tested in the same way that other types of beliefs and associations should be tested—in terms of their effects in the natural world, of which the social world is a part, in which we all live. Our natural world is a world in which methods of inquiry based on more than 350 years of successes in experimental, peer-reviewed sciences can be utilized to promote learning from early to late, fostering the growth of individuals and societies, through the course of an entire lifetime. In all of this, Dewey has provided a tool kit for the maintenance of democratic forms of life.

Notes

1. For an account of one of the more outrageous attempts by the Bush administration to rewrite scientific reports to reflect its own ideology, see "Top-Level Editing on Climate Issues," *The New York Times*, June 8, 2005, A1.

2. Since this paragraph was written, in 2005, the number of signers has greatly increased. They now number more than 11,000, including "52 Nobel laureates, 63 National Medal of Science recipients, and 195 members of the National Academies." See the entire list at http://www.ucsusa.org/scientific_integrity/restoring/. Retrieved April 25, 2007.

3. For a discussion of the distinction between physicalism and materialism, see an excellent article in the *Stanford Encyclopedia of Philosophy*, February 13, 2001, at http://www.plato.stanford.edu/entries/physicalism/. Retrieved April 22, 2007.

4. There is, of course, an exception that has been called "the pragmatic a priori." An a priori truth in this sense is not necessary *überhaupt*, but necessary *for*. This type of a priori prescribes nothing to experience. See Lewis (1970, 231–39).

Works Cited

Adler, M. 1977. This prewar generation (1940). In *Reforming education*, ed. Geraldine Van Doren, New York: Macmillan.

Duff, M. 2002. Evolution challenged in US schools. *BBC News*. March 11. Retrieved April 21, 2007.

Lewis, C. I. 1970. A pragmatic conception of the *a priori*. In *Collected papers of Clarence Irving Lewis*, ed. John D. Goheen and John L. Mothershead, Jr., 231–239, Stanford, CA: Stanford University Press.

Margolis, J. 2002. *Reinventing pragmatism*. Ithaca, NY: Cornell University Press.

Plantinga, A. 1998. Methodological naturalism part 2. *Acess Research Network: Origins & Design*, 18:2, (January 1) http://www.arn.org/docs/odesign/od182/methnat182.htm. Retrieved April 21, 2007.

Poll: 2004. Creationism trumps evolution.*CBS News*. November 22. http://www.cbsnews.com/stories/2004/11/22/opinion/polls/main657083.shtml. Retrieved April 21, 2007.

Ruse, M. 2001. *Can a Darwinian be a Christian?* Cambridge: Cambridge University Press.

Savage, Dan. 2005. The gay child left behind. *The New York Times*. February 17, A27.

Chapter 6

Thinking Desire: Taking Perspectives Seriously

Charlene Haddock Seigfried

Unlike the hypertextuality and linguistic-centeredness of so much current theorizing, pragmatist philosophy begins with experience and explores the ways that thought, language, and theory emerge from and merge with it. In Charles Sanders Peirce's words: "Experience is our only teacher" (1934, 37).[1] But other philosophical traditions also have claimed to be experientially based. British empiricism, one of the historical antecedents to pragmatism, immediately comes to mind, as well as the immediate intuitionism of analytic philosophy that gains its credibility from the supposed indubitability of intuitions or subjective feelings. It is both the way that experience is understood—as an activity of experiencing, for example, rather than experience as a discrete kind or class and as a transaction encompassing both organism and environment, rather than referring only to the subjective side—as well as the consequences that are drawn from experience so understood that distinguishes the pragmatist perspective from other traditions that appeal to experience.

The aspect of experience that I will be examining is what William James means by selective interest, according to which practical and aesthetic interests are the "irreducible ultimate factors in determining the way our knowledge grows" (1983a, 16). Of the various practical interests he describes, the relationship of reality to ourselves will be emphasized (James 1982, 919, n. 7).[2] It is what John Dewey refers to in his postulate "that things—anything, everything, in the ordinary or non-technical use of the term 'thing'—are what they are experienced as. Hence, if one wishes to describe anything truly, his task is to tell what it is experienced as being" (MW 3: 158). He is at pains to emphasize that what something is experienced as is not reducible to what it is known as, knowledge being just one approach to or aspect of a qualitatively rich having-to-do-with. He also is aware that "philosophers, in common with theologians and social theorists, are as sure that personal habits and interests shape their opponents' doctrines as they are that their own beliefs are absolutely universal and objective in quality" and blames this self-serving myopia for the "dishonesty, that insincerity characteristic of philosophic discussion" (MW 4: 113). Moreover, as the flourishing of feminist, black, multicultural, and other perspective-based philosophies has confirmed, he correctly predicted that "the moment the complicity of the personal factor in our philosophic valuations is recognized, is recognized fully, frankly and generally, that moment a new era in philosophy will begin" (ibid.). This new era has already begun, as chapters by Garrison, Reich, Neubert, and Green in this book demonstrate. Dewey chides Aristotle for elevating pure, passionless cognition over "thinking desire," Aristotle's own term for practical knowledge. Unlike the passionless reason of pure knowledge, "[t]hinking desire is experimental, is tentative, not absolute. It looks to the future, and to the past for help in the future. It is contingent, not necessary. It doubly relates to the individual: to the individual thing as experienced by an individual agent" (MW 3: 89). In this chapter, I focus on some consequences that flow from the fact that all experiencing occurs to someone at some when and somewhere.

Since this perspectival character of experience cannot be eliminated, what are we to think of it, and how are we to deal with it? As James says of some particularly absorbent containers, or perhaps of some particularly odorous substances, you can rinse and rinse a bottle and not get rid of the taste of its first contents. But we sometimes operate as if we could cleanse our experientially based theories of all traces of their origins, as if we could leave the original or supporting perspectives behind and just deal with the facts of experience as facts. It seems to me that too much pragmatist theorizing pays lip service to perspectivalism and then operates as if it could safely be ignored, as if it did not affect every aspect of our experiential analyses. Pragmatists too easily move from the subjective apprehensions of experience to objective claims about reality without exploring the peculiar character of the objectivity obtainable from context-specific experiences.

Peirce, for example, clarifies his claim about experience by asking how this action of experience takes place and answering: "It takes place by a series of surprises." Surprises are unexpected occurrences. This could be interpreted to mean that the fact that our expectations are not always met is evidence for the coercive force of the objects that we experience and the independence of the laws of nature. It would then be well for my desires to take account of what is disclosed in order to avoid arbitrariness. Although we may not be able to directly apprehend the nature of reality, we can come closer and closer to grasping it as a result of repeated experiments. Peirce's belief in the eventual convergence of experimental findings seems to support an understanding of experience in which perspectives are eventually overcome as the universal truths are grasped. He says: "This final opinion, then, is independent, not indeed of thought in general, but of all that is arbitrary and individual in thought; it is quite independent of how you, or I, or any number of men think."[3]

The pragmatist understanding of experience that I am developing is as far from this assertion that feelings, idiosyncrasies, and intentions are left behind when experience is stripped of its subjectivity in attaining "thought in general" as empiricism is from radical empiricism, or what Dewey calls "critical radical empiricism."[4] It is radical "in the sense that it recognizes the claims and traits of all qualitative modes and organizations of experience, instead of setting up some one form as ultimate and 'real'; critical, in that each philosophy is interpreted not in terms of abstract criteria of truth and value (a method which of necessity begs the question), but of concrete historic origin, context and operation" (MW 13: 353). The pragmatists trust experience to yield those ends-in-view capable of guiding us to a better way of life. A big-picture metaphysics, such as Green envisions in this book, would be neither critical nor radical in the concrete, contextual, historical, and operational sense just given. Even if it is granted that Green is redefining metaphysics to fit these qualifications, it seems superfluous and misleading to call such an approach a metaphysics rather than a critical, radically empiricist method. Both Hans Seigfried and Hickman argue that democratic social inquiry is best undertaken by adopting principles of inquiry that are strictly experimental and functional.[5] Like Dewey and James, Sara Ruddick believes that such "[c]oncreteness is opposed to 'abstraction'—a cluster of interrelated dispositions to simplify, generalize, and sharply define. To look and then speak concretely is to relish complexity, tolerate ambiguity, to multiply options rather than accepting the terms of the problem" (1989, 93).

The ability to relish complexity and tolerate ambiguity is exemplified in Henry James's work as he patiently adds stroke after stroke of multiple perspectives to gradually build up various worlds of experience. His writings show that he was acutely aware of the perspectival character of experience and the persuasiveness of the conclusions reached on the basis of it. In 1904, for example, he returned to America after an absence of twenty-one years and recorded his impressions of his native land in *The American Scene*. A continuing theme throughout the book is how his "prompt reactions" to some aspects of the passing scene and his "imperturbable inertness" to others made the travelogue an inner journey, one in which he could explore his sense of self as both an "initiated native" and an "inquiring stranger." But the passing scene revealed more to him than the self he had become in the interim; his responses elicited hitherto unrealized aspects of American life. In the preface he states what amounts to a manifesto when he says that, despite some possible blind spots, "I would take my stand on my gathered impressions" (1994, 3). Like his brother William, James chipped away at the assumption of transparent access to objects as they are in themselves by stressing the different realms of reality that appear from different points of view. He denies that experienced objects are less truly understood because grasped only from a limited angle of vision and expresses "confidence in the objective reality of impressions" and marvels how the many impressions bombarding him as he passed through the New Jersey countryside "were at the mercy of observation" (8–9).

According to William James, too, the simply given order of reality is too overwhelming (he variously terms it a chaos or a much-at-onceness) to be grasped except by transforming "the world of our impressions into a totally different world—the world of our conception." But the relation of concepts to percepts and their specific differences are well-worn themes in philosophy and not worth remarking on except for the way James focuses on the claim of total difference between the two worlds and draws out unforeseen consequences. He insists that this transformation is effected solely *"for the sake of ends* that do not exist at all in the world of impressions we receive by way of our senses," and by so doing, he—like Nietzsche—exaggerates the chasm between sensory impression and the concepts or ideas based on them (James, 1979, 94–95; see Nietzsche, 1882/1974, sections 57–58, emphasis in original). Our ideas may very well be the ideas of the objects perceived by our senses, but such objects are only objects in view of the ends we have in mind. Given other ends, other objects or realities would be as indubitably perceived. Moreover, by such ends, James does not mean the intention to get the world just right or to obtain the truth about reality or to faithfully mirror in some symbolic sense what our senses perceive, because the ends, goals, or intentions through which experiences are constituted "are set by our emotional and practical subjectivity altogether." Lest he be misunderstood, he quite bluntly says, "We have no organ or faculty to appreciate the simply given order." We cannot even think "the real world as it is given objectively," but only as it is taken by us, subjectively (James 1979, 94–95).

Feelings, emotions, and practical wants and needs are the very pivot on which subjective experience turns into objective claims. Nietzsche also gives as the essence of this perspectival view the fact that "all our actions are altogether incomparably personal, unique, and infinitely individual;... but as soon as we

translate them into consciousness they no longer seem to be"
([1882] 1974, 354). Objectivity is a certain sort of subjectivity,
not its opposite. Subjective determinations are coercive. As
James starkly claims: "The preferences of sentient crea-
tures...are the absolute and ultimate law-giver here" (1979,
194). Our purposes or intentions select the world to which we
pay attention and therefore operate in and make claims about.
Our feelings also determine the moral realm according to
James, who says that "[i]f we were radically feelingless,...we
would lose all our likes and dislikes at a stroke" and along with
them any means of finding any situation or experience more
valuable than another (1983b, 132). Such feelings and selective
interests identify who we are as persons. Emotions and feelings
are highly valuable aspects of experience, because they are
expressions of that creativity, of the power to weave order out of
the chaos that makes up a large share of what it is to be a
person. As such, pragmatists often emphasize the function and
value of feelings.

James expected that our multitude of moral, aesthetic, and
practical desires would never succumb to the mental barbarism
of scientific reductionism, despite its increasing hegemony. The
reason is that our active and emotional tendencies disclose
aspects of the world not available to scientific methodology. In
fact, our chief difference from other animal species lies precisely
in the excessive number and variety of our desires. James warned
that an excessive zeal for scientific rationality will have the
unforeseen consequence of "blighting the development of the
intellect itself quite as much as that of the feelings or the will"
(1979, 104). This is because even our scientific or rational
demands for clarity, simplicity, and coherence stem from the
excess of our desires over simply recording the world around us
or developing logically consistent systems. The heuristics of
accurate sense representation and noncontradictory explanations
are themselves a result of spontaneous, irrational demands.
James goes so far as to claim that had man's "whole life not been
a quest for the superfluous, he would never have established
himself as inexpugnably as he has in the necessary" (ibid.).

James calls on us to oppose the increasing dominance of
"the appetite for immediate consistency at any cost, or what the

logicians call the "law of parsimony." More than ever, we need to deliberately defend those forms of being that our emotional and active tendencies alone give us access to. Otherwise, to the extent that philosophy reduces itself to these purely rational norms, it will be increasingly ignored by the public and will continue down the path already well worn by medieval scholasticism, namely, saying less and less ever more precisely. Of a male-gendered discipline of philosophy, James warns, "Prune down his extravagance, sober him, and you undo him" (ibid.). The apparent extravagance of the increasing numbers of women and "racially" diverse philosophers *has* shaken up the sober discipline of philosophy, but it might also—as James predicted—be a means of reawakening interest in the multitude of desires shunted aside in favor of a narrow, ever more arcane conception of rationality.

But feelings—subjective attitudes—also considerably complicate our ability to achieve consensus on claims about the meaning of experience and the nature of reality. The multiplicity of ends set by our emotional and practical subjectivity has to be brought into a working relationship with one another for a sense of self to emerge and stabilize, for meaningful communication to take place among persons, and to enable people to live together amicably. We always fall short of these goals, however, because of the irreducibility of individual feelings. According to James, values are rooted in personal feelings, and every concrete person puts forth moral claims that de facto create obligations. But because it is impossible in the world that we inhabit to satisfy all claims, some must be butchered so that others can be fulfilled (154–55). The word "butchered" expresses James's revulsion at this practical necessity. It is a tribute to his consistency in closely linking feelings to persons, with all of the idiosyncratic uniqueness this implies, that James denies the possibility of the usual philosophic move to appeal to a common essence in all moral judgments or to a universal rule to resolve the conflict of values present and operative in the world. To choose any one of these criteria among the many proposed by different philosophers—from Aristotle's mean between two extremes or Kant's categorical imperative—would be to favor one person's preferences over many others. It would deny the intimate link between preference and value that he has been arguing for and that he calls "the *most* universal principle," namely, "that *the essence of good is simply to satisfy demand*" (153, emphasis in original). In trying to satisfy the preferences of as many persons as possible, some will inevitably not be provided for. Since this does not diminish their obligatory force, their anguish at being rejected should call out to us anew to find some creative way to accommodate them also or at another time or in another situation.

As Henry James, "the restless analyst" of *The American Scene*, minutely analyzes his responses to a confusing variety of situations, he seems intent on demonstrating William James's claim that our conceptions of what is taking place "characterize *us* more than they characterize the thing" (1982, 961). Nonetheless, they *do* characterize things, and Henry James fears that the diminished view of America that he feels after many years abroad just might be a true reflection of what America has become. Feelings are our feelers, guiding us through the experienced world. But as much as they reveal, they conceal, and this aspect of subjectivity, by which our understanding and experiences are limited, is not lost on the early pragmatists. Henry James says that such "selection and omission . . . become almost a pain" (1994, 13) in the same sense in which William James laments over conceptualization always involving selecting some aspects of reality and ignoring others: "I am always unjust, always partial, always exclusive" (1994, 960).[6] If such partiality and unfairness are built into the very nature of experience, as the pragmatists claim, then their worldview is less sanguine than it at first seems to be.

If feelings cannot be eliminated from our understanding of the world, then they have to be taken account of in efforts to find intelligible ways to make claims about reality and decisions about how to handle it. We know the harms that have been caused by the injustice of deliberately oppressive points of view. William James also recognizes and abhors the sufferings inflicted by evil actions, so although he argues that good cannot be detached from desires or demands, he cannot literally mean that all demands ought to be met.[7] But if we can operate in the world only insofar as we select some aspects of it and reject others, then merely having nonoppressive intentions cannot eliminate the unfairness of the process. Can the unintended yet sometimes harmful effects of such partiality be mitigated, if not fully eliminated? The pragmatists think so, and one way they take account of feelings is in formulating the pragmatic method. Dewey urges the use of the pragmatic method as a powerful tool capable of dealing with the clash of preferences and hence of values. But it should be remembered that the method itself only operates correctly insofar as the subjective aspect of experience is integrated into its workings. The ubiquity of feelings in experience explains why Dewey begins with the indeterminate situation and calls the first step of the pragmatic method the instantiation of the problem, rather than beginning with the formulation of hypotheses for resolving a given problem. Until the parameters of the problem have been reflectively determined in a way amenable to further inquiry, even intensely felt problems are initial conditions, the material of problematic situations, which are driven by multiple feelings and desires.

We need to understand how the problematic situation has come to be problematic from many and various points of view. It is too glib to say that the first step of the pragmatic method is working out just what the problem is that is causing trouble. As Neubert and Reich also indicate, we need to delve more deeply into what such "working out" means.[8] It means at least to enlarge the context, to learn of its relations to other, similar problems, and to find available sources of knowledge already gained from the way that something like the present situation has been problematized and solutions developed in the past. But it also means that we need to pay attention to the different feelings and passions that have led to the conflicts that are a large part of the problematic nature of problematic situations. It should not surprise us when heightened emotions disrupt the exercise of the pragmatic method in efforts to solve socially significant problems. According to Dewey, emotional states that constitute the pervasive quality of experience become distinctively emotional insofar as they "become parts of an inclusive and enduring situation that involves concern for objects and their issues" (LW 10: 49). Disturbing social situations of sufficient significance as to require the use of the pragmatic method certainly involve that concern for objects and their issues that brings out the distinctively emotional.

In his more rigorous explication of the pragmatic method in his 1938 *Logic*, Dewey recognizes that personal emotions actively contribute to the production of ideas and beliefs. They inevitably "cook the evidence and determine the result that is reached." But he acknowledges "the part played in human judgments by emotion and desire," only to banish them from the logic of inquiry, since "[t]o be intellectually 'objective' is to discount and eliminate merely personal factors in the operations by which a conclusion is reached" (LW 12: 50). This separation of merely personal emotions and desires from intellectual inquiry is not so draconian as it sounds, however. Dewey is concerned to break through the organic and cultural limitations of personal emotions and experiences so that persons can take the standpoint of other participants in the conjoint undertaking of inquiry. Communication among differently situated persons would otherwise be blocked before it even got started. Whether such "preparatory responsiveness" succeeds in forging communicative links to common understanding can only be fully determined in the actual transformation of existing conditions that constitutes the experimental method (51–65). There is nothing wrong with the broad outline of Dewey's explanation of the cultural factors involved in the existential matrix of inquiry, which we have been considering. However, he dismisses too easily the role played by emotions, both in the initial formulation of the problematic situation and in the eventual outcome of inquiry. More needs to be said, for instance, about how the very emotions that color observation and judgment to such an extent that they can be said to cook the evidence would also not be carried over into perceiving and evaluating the conclusions reached in experimental inquiry.

The role of emotion in inquiry that Dewey has slighted has been extensively developed by feminists.[9] Judith A. Cook, for example, points out that a "major feature of feminist epistemology is its refusal to ignore the emotional dimension of the conduct of inquiry...emotions serve as a source of insight or a signal of rupture in social reality" (cited in Fornow and Cook, 1991, 9). And Annette Baier calls Hume "the woman's moral philosopher," because he held that "corrected (sometimes rule-corrected) sympathy, not law-discerning reason, is the fundamental moral capacity."[10] The methods of consciousness-raising developed by feminists in the 1960s explored in depth the many ways that feelings and expectations can reveal important aspects of situations but also can serve to block and distort communication. These insights have been developed further in feminist psychology and anthropology, both to explain the ways that racist, classist, and other feelings unconsciously influence perceptions and to develop methods for taking them into account and dealing with them (see Fonow and Cook 1991, 3-4).

In her many writings, Jane Addams shows how feelings and preconceptions operate in experience and can either hinder or help communication, the process of gaining knowledge, and the resolution of pressing social problems (1910). In the midst of the First World War, for example, she reported that delegates to the International Congress of Women at the Hague thought that one of the factors contributing to the failure of peace efforts to prevent the war may have been that appeals had been "made too exclusively to reason and a sense of justice, that reason is only a part of the human endowment," and that emotion and deep-set human impulses must be utilized as well. These include the basic human urge "to foster life and to protect the helpless, of which women were the earliest custodians, and even the social and gregarious instincts that we share with the animals themselves" (Addams 1915, 130–31). Given the postmodernist feminist interest in the political repercussions of affectivity, especially Luce Irigaray's call for "a critical reappraisal of the notion of desire itself," Addams's further remarks take on renewed resonance: "These universal desires must be given opportunities to expand and to have a recognized place in the formal organization of international relations which, up to this moment, have rested so exclusively upon purely legal foundations" (130).

Having recognized the role of desires in human activity, a means must be found to critically appraise them. According to Dewey, "[w]e shall have to discover the personal factors that now influence us unconsciously, and begin to accept a new and moral responsibility for them, a responsibility for judging and testing them by their consequences. So long as we ignore this factor, its deeds will be largely evil, not because it is evil, but because, flourishing in the dark, it is without responsibility and without check. The only way to control it is by recognizing it" (MW 4: 113–14). Addams also demonstrated the role of feelings in experience and the need to critically reflect on their influence by elaborating on her discovery that in the work that she and other women undertook at Hull House, large and generous feelings had been too broadly or too vaguely articulated. To do good, to be generous to the poor, to stop war, and to prevent the exploitation of workers, children, immigrants, and the elderly may all be laudable aims. But as soon as such intentions, with their attendant feelings, were brought to bear on specific social problems, the settlement workers often became perplexed because their proposals were resisted and sometimes even resented by those they were intended to help.[11] Puzzling over this state of affairs led to the realization that in such inter-changes, Addams and the other women often unconsciously brought with them feelings of racial, cultural, class, or religious superiority. Without their awareness, these feelings were shap-ing and misshaping the situation. The recipients of their atten-tions also brought their own feelings and beliefs to the situation, ones that also both illuminated and distorted the situ-ation and the discussions taking place. It was only by acknowl-edging and articulating these feelings and perceptions that they could be worked through as part of dealing with the problems at hand.

In recognizing the privilege of dominant perspectives and working to overcome its effects, Addams illuminates the power of feelings to shape situations.[12] She also recognizes that when feelings and passions conflict, a way must be found to acknowl-edge perspectives that we do not share, otherwise we run the risk of blindly asserting what seems obvious from our point of view and of failing to recognize our own hidden biases. Rather than denying the validity of the feelings and vested interests of ward bosses, saloon keepers, factory owners, and corrupt politi-cians, for example, Addams saw the need to figure out why they obviously felt good about their role in creating situations that so obviously hurt many others (2002). What feels good to the dominant side feels abhorrent to their victims, who in turn feel benefits in situations the other side avoids assiduously. In a similar manner, Richard Rorty recommends that instead of treating those who offend our moral sensibilities "as irrational, we should treat them as deprived" (1998, 180). What they are deprived of is enough security so that those who differ from them by race or ethnicity, religion, gender, or sexual preference will not be perceived of as threatening their own way of life. They also are deprived of or lacking in enough sympathy to identify with the harms suffered by these alien others. This is a significant failure since, according to Rorty, pragmatists "substitute the idea of a maximally warm, sensitive and sympathetic human being for the Kantian idea of a Good Will" (1999, 83). Addams thinks that both sides can learn from the other, but only if each is willing to acknowledge its own limitations. This does not mean that prejudiced attitudes and the harmful actions that follow from them cannot be condemned. It does mean that for oppressive situations to be transformed into emancipatory ones over the long haul, both sides will need to be convinced of the value of such a transformation, and this requires more than condemnation. It requires figuring out what it takes for persons or groups who draw the boundaries of their sympathetic understanding too narrowly at their own national, ethnic, class, or gender identities to broaden them.[13]

Dewey further explains his claim that to be a human being is to be thinking desire by asserting that "the agreement of desires is not in oneness of intellectual conclusion, but in the sympathies of passion and the concords of action—and yet significant union in affection and behavior may depend upon a consensus in thought that is secured only by discrimination and comparison" (MW 3: 100.). In regard to the tragic events that took place in Rwanda and the former Yugoslavia, for example, we can ask such questions as these: What were the passions that led to ethnic cleansing? Why is it that feelings of loyalty to one's own ethnic group can lead to lethal feelings toward perceived outsiders? What arouses these passions, and what can be done about them? As the increasing number of terrorist attacks all over the world since the ones in New York, Pennsylvania, and Washington, D.C., all too vividly reminds us, the animosity expressed among ethnic or religious groups and the horrific actions that took place as a result are unfortunately not isolated cases, limited to Rwanda or the former Yugoslavia. It is not enough to stop the violence by force in one place, only to have it break out again in another. We know that both ethnic cleansing and terrorist attacks, on the one hand, and living in harmony with those who differ from us in significant ways, on the other hand, have been desired by various peoples at various times. It is also only too obvious that both are not equally desirable. What is not so well recognized is that the desirable cannot be obtained and sustained without going through desires, however problematic.

Addams gradually came to realize that we are not only ignorant of what others desire but often despise it when we do know. Thus it is not enough to see the world as others see it, however important this is as a first step to any long-lasting resolution of antagonisms. The overwhelming desire to strike back after being attacked is vividly illustrated by the actions of the U.S. government in response to the destruction of the World Trade Center towers. That the perpetrators were not the forward edge of an assault by one country on another did not dampen the desire for revenge or overcome feelings of vulnerability, but only inflamed them. In the absence of a clear, identifiable enemy target, one was quickly assembled out of bits and pieces of past slights, disappointments, hurt pride, and smoldering grudges. Which emotionally pervaded facts and values are strong enough to counter appeals to our baser emotions in the service of an economic-political-military juggernaut? And even if there are any, how can they be accepted by those whose thinking desires run strongly counter to them? There is no easy answer to this problem, as various European leaders found in their attempts to persuade the United States to take a more moderate approach to Iraq. We can only keep trying to find ways to break down the barriers set up by our diverse nationalistic, gender, ethnic, class, sexual, and religious situatednesses.

Passions and emotions play a large role in perpetrating attacks on perceived enemies, help rigidify oppressive attitudes, and stymie attempts to resolve conflicts. Think of the efforts of the Bush administration in the United States to control the images being sent back during the Iraq War by embedding reporters within military units, thus both controlling their movements and slyly bonding them to their companion soldiers. The emotional pull of wartime images is not underrated by members of Bush's war council, who can remember the growing disenchantment with the Vietnam War because of the spontaneous revulsion many people felt when they witnessed— directly or via the media—the maiming and killing of women, children, and other unarmed civilians, even when they were officially labeled enemy collaborators or dismissed as the unintended consequences of legitimate military targets. As such calculated steps to support the war effort through controlled images unwittingly demonstrate, passions and emotions also can be allies in communicating suppressed points of view and reaching more amicable results. Because they can operate below or outside of the control of conscious beliefs and ideology, emotions can be subversive. Besides the unintentional effects emotions can exert, they also can be deliberately aroused and channeled by indoctrination or strongly held beliefs, as in the deliberate raping or killing of civilians by combatants in wartime, but also in arousing others to oppose and stop such horrific actions.

Emotions, therefore, are deeply problematic, but so are other components of knowledge and values, such as sense data, illusions, and ethnocentrism. Pragmatists contend that emotions do not just accompany, follow, impede, distort, motivate, or dislodge knowledge and values—they help constitute them. We have seen how this claim is a result of beginning reflection with experience, and for pragmatists experience includes both what is experienced and how it is experienced. To critically engage such a state of affairs, experience also is used methodologically.[14] It must be critically appropriated if it is to be effective in producing warranted knowledge. In contrast to theories that assume the passionless and empty reason of pure knowledge, theories such as pragmatism, which begin with a recognition of the central role of thinking desire in human experience, adopt an attitude that is experimental, tentative, and nonabsolute.[15] Pragmatist theory operates within a horizon of temporality and thus looks to the future and to the past for help in the future. Its conclusions are contingent and not necessary. Most

importantly, it is anti-essentialist and nonreductive, and it recognizes and responds to the partiality of individuals in interaction with their environment.

Notes

1. See also McDermott (1976, 17).

2. See also Seigfried (1990, 121–25).

3. Peirce, in Schneider (1963, 437).

4. For radical empiricism, see "William James," in Kim and Sosa.
(1995). For critical radical empiricism, see Dewey (MW13:353).

5. See Hans Seigfried's chapter, in this book for how Dewey's
experimentalism or instrumentalism displaces the need for a metaphysical framework to provide guidance. Also see Hickman, in this
book: "What this means in practice is that [Dewey's] theory of inquiry
rejects a priorisms in general, it treats metaphysical, epistemological,
and theological presuppositions not as foundations to be shoved *under*
inquiry, as it were, but as hypotheses to be examined *by* inquiry in
order to determine whether they are warranted and assertible."

6. According to Nietzsche (1882/1974), "Whatever becomes conscious becomes by the same token shallow, thin, relatively stupid, general, sign, herd signal; all becoming conscious involves a great and
thorough corruption, falsification, reduction to superficialities, and
generalization" (section 354).

7. It is difficult to reconcile James's ultimate universal principle,
that the essence of good is simply to satisfy demand, and his naturalistic account in *The Principles of Psychology*, of a hierarchy of goods that
ought to characterize persons. One possibility is to argue for an evolutionary model of moral development in which a proliferation of valued
ways of life is to be preferred over a forced uniformity. On this view,
the nature of good is not arrived at a priori or through rational deduc-
tion but only after someone actually states a preference and makes a
claim, and the consequences of agreeing to that claim turn out better
than not doing so.

8. In discussing the three metaperspectives earlier in this book,
Neubert specifies the multilayered cultural contexts of social interactions and shows how Dewey underestimated the continuing influence
of the multiple ways we encounter the world, while Reich develops

two important omissions in Dewey's discussions of criteria for education toward representative democracy.

9. For connections between the two, see Seigfried (2002b).

10. Quoted in Rorty (1998, 180–81).

11. On the role of the feeling of perplexity in Addams's methodology of inquiry, see Seigfried (2002a, xxii–xxxi).

12. In his contribution to this book, Garrison gives the example of "emotional dismissal" as one particularly disturbing example of how dominant perspectives can completely take over and entirely define a situation to such a degree that all other perspectives are simply eliminated. He rightly argues that these public uses of emotions, which usually are ignored as merely subjective, need to be addressed because of their political impact. His integration of feminist theory into his chapter is appreciated.

13. For Jane Addams's principle of sympathetic understanding, see Seigfried (2007).

14. See Hickman's chapter in this book and Hans Seigfried's chapter on Dewey's historical or evolutionary method as a better basis for moral theory than ones based on inductive generalization because it emphasizes the process by which what is morally valued is analyzed in concrete, emerging contexts and determined to be morally valuable within those contexts.

15. See Seigfried (2003, 35).

Works Cited

Addams, J. 1910. *Twenty years at Hull-House*. New York: Macmillan.
———. 1915. Women and internationalism. In *Women at the Hague*, ed. E. Addams, G. Balch, and A. Hamilton, New York: Macmillan.
———. 2002. *Democracy and social ethics*. Urbana and Chicago: University of Illinois Press.
Cook, J. A. 1988. Who mothers the chronically mentally ill? *Family Relations* 37: 42–49.

Fonow, M. M., and J. A. Cook, eds. 1991. *Beyond methodology: Feminist scholarship as lived research*. Bloomington and Indianapolis: Indiana University Press.

James, H. 1994. *The American scene*. New York: Penguin Books.

James, W. 1979. *The will to believe*. Cambridge, MA: Harvard University Press.

———. 1982. *The principles of psychology, vol. II*. Cambridge, MA: Harvard University Press.

———. James, W. 1983a. *Essays in Psychology*. Cambridge, MA: Harvard University Press.

———. 1983b. On a certain blindness in human beings. In *Talks to Teachers*, Cambridge, MA: Harvard University Press, 149–169.

Kim, J., and E. Sosa, eds. 1995. *A companion to metaphysics*. Oxford: Basil Blackwell.

McDermott, J. J. 1976. *The culture of experience*. New York: New York University Press.

Nietzsche, F. [1882] 1974. *The gay science*. Edited by Walter Kaufmann. New York: Vintage Books.

Peirce, C. S. 1934. *Collected papers*, vol. 5. Edited by Charles Hartshorne and Paul Weiss. Cambridge, MA: Harvard University Press.

Rorty, R. 1998. Human rights, rationality, and sentimentality. In *Truth and progress: Philosophical Papers, vol. 3* ed., Cambridge: Cambridge University Press, 167–185.

———. 1999. *Philosophy and social hope*. New York: Penguin Books.

Ruddick, S. 1989. *Maternal thinking: Toward a politics of peace*. New York: Ballantine Books.

Schneider, H. W. 1963. *A history of American philosophy*. 2d ed. New York: Columbia University Press.

Seigfried, C. H. 1990. *William James's radical reconstruction of philosophy*. Albany: State University of New York Press.

———. Introduction. 2002a. In *Democracy and social ethics*, in Addams, 2002.

———. 2002b John Dewey's pragmatist feminism. In *Feminist interpretations of John Dewey*, ed. Charlene Haddock Seigfried, 47–77. University Park: Pennsylvania State University Press.

Seigfried, 2003. "Has passion a place in philosophy?" in Robert Audi, ed. Philosophy in America at the Turn of the Century. APA Centennial Supplement, *Journal of Philosophical Research*. Charlottesville, VA: Philosophy Documentation Center, 2003. 35–54.

———. 2007. Learning from experience: Jane Addams's education in democracy as a way of life. In *Ethical visions of education: philosophies in practice*, ed. David T. Hansen, 83–94. New York: Teachers College Press.

Chapter 7

A Pragmatist Approach to Emotional Expression and the Construction of Gender Identity

Jim Garrison

This chapter examines dominant sociocultural interpretations of emotional expression for clues to the construction of social identity, especially gender identity. I rely considerably on Shannon Sullivan's feminist reconstruction of Dewey's notion of "body-minds." I supplement this reconstruction with some of my own work on Dewey's theory of emotions and emotional interpretation concentrating on what is right, and wrong, with Paul Ekman's cross-cultural studies of automatic "affect program" responses and socioculturally mediated "display rules" that override or mask affect response programs. We will find that while these responses are perhaps innate, what they respond to is culturally contingent. I concentrate on a failed instance of cross-gender communication in a school setting in the United States that involves what Sue Campbell calls "being dismissed" emotionally and what it means for female gender construction. For Dewey, personal identity, rights, and freedom are contingent social constructions, the quest of a lifetime for

every individual, and an achievement of a culture across genera-
tions. Such things are not natural endowments, as classical
democratic liberals would have it. I conclude with a discussion of
Dewey's idea that intelligence, not free will, is the key to freedom in action. This chapter seeks to call attention to the embodied affective aspect of communicative democracy by illustrating
what can go wrong in dialogues across the kinds of differences
discussed by Reich, Neubert, Haddock Seigfried, and others in
this book, and what we might do about it.

Sullivan's (2001) wonderfully insightful book "presents an
account of corporeal existence as transactional" and emphasizes
"the dynamic, co-constitutive relationship of organisms and
their environments" wherein the "boundaries that delimit individual entities are permeable, not fixed, which means that
organisms and their various environments—social, cultural, and
political as well as physical—are constituted by their mutual
influence and impact on each other" (1). Sullivan's emphasis is
on what she calls the gendered "bodying" of "body-minds." She
states: "How body-minds create meaning has implications for
the constitution of gender, and Dewey's notion of habit is crucial to understanding gendered existence, including the possibility of reconfiguration" (9). Embodied beings inhabit their
world, as Haddock Seigfried showed clearly in the last chapter.

A central feature of Sullivan's book is the realization that
there are no pure prediscursive body-minds. Sullivan builds on
and surpasses the work of Judith Butler (1990, 1993, 1997).
Both recognize that participating in sociolinguistic practices
transforms psycho-physical beings into body-minds with meaningful emotions, thoughts, and actions.[1] Said differently, the
emotions, thoughts, and actions of all body-minds are interpreted not only by others but also by themselves. It is worth
remembering that, for Dewey, "Meanings are rules for using
and interpreting things; interpretation being always an imputation of potentiality for some consequence" (LW 1: 147).
Sullivan and I are interested in what happens when someone
feels their actions are misinterpreted, especially their emotional
actions, by the dominant culture.

Sullivan explores how the customary norms inscribe themselves on body-minds. She states: "Like gender, sex is a norma-

tive cultural sedimentation that regulates bodies" (2001, 59).
These norms impose themselves upon body-minds by condi-
tioning habits of social conduct. For Dewey, we acquire meanings, and thereby our minds, by participating in the
norm-governed social practices of a culture. Meaning emerges
between two or more emergent body-minds when they can
come to an agreement in action regarding the consequence of
some emerging object codesignated in the social transaction.
When two or more persons mutually agree on the potentiality
for various consequences of some meaning (e.g., idea, ideal,
object) cointended between them, they creatively make meaning and come to a mutual understanding, even if they do not
agree about the truth or value of the consequences. We also
must remember that "meanings are rules for using and interpreting things, interpretation being always an imputation of
potentiality for some consequence" (LW 1: 147). This chapter
concentrates on disagreement over interpretation.

The interpretation of our thoughts, feelings, and actions by
others and ourselves depends on norms of "proper" and compe-
tent comportment. Sullivan links habits and normativity to
Butler's notion of stylized gender performativity:

> Habit is an organism's constitutive predisposition to transact
> with the world in particular ways, and performativity is the
> process of repetitive activity that constitutively stylizes one's
> being. Together, these ideas provide powerful tools with which
> to understand the composition and transformation of gender.
> (2001, 88)

The customary norms of culture impart distinctive ways of "bodying," allowing us to carry out distinct, stylized performances.

Let us rely directly on Dewey to explore how embodying
cultural norms leads to stylized performances. Dewey begins
Human Nature and Conduct with the chapter "Habits as Social
Functions." The chapter opens by asserting, "Habits may be
profitably compared to physiological functions" (MW 14: 15).
So comprehended, "natural operations like breathing and
digesting, acquired ones like speech and honesty, are functions
of the surroundings as truly as of a person. They are things

done by the environment by means of organic structures or acquired dispositions.... [F]unctions and habits are ways of using and incorporating the environment in which the latter has its say as surely as the former" (15). As social functions, habits incorporate the social environment into themselves, hence, habits are not simply located inside of the body.

We acquire our habits from our habitat, especially the norms and customs of our social habitat. For the most part, "individuals form their personal habits under conditions set by prior customs" (43). Initially, the customs of the culture in whose social practices we participate largely determine our personal identity. Different cultures and subcultures impart different habits, beliefs for interpreting the world. Members of different cultures, subcultures, races, ethnicities, and genders acquire different patterns of selective attention and habitual response to the world. To some degree, they occupy different worlds. Dewey insists that "habits endure, because these habits incorporate objective conditions in themselves" (19). He further indicates that "all habits are affections," and that all "habits are demands for certain kinds of activity; and they constitute the self.... [T]hey are will" (21). Habits have an affective as well as a cognitive component that governs action. Habits organize and structure otherwise free-floating feelings. Finally, habits enable stylized performances, because "habits are arts" that "involve skill of sensory and motor organs, cunning or craft, and objective materials" (15). Habits provide skilled "know-how."

Sullivan mentions embodied, unconscious "knowing how" to walk properly in high-heeled shoes, her middle-class tendency to smile often when conversing with others, and keeping her knees together when seated.[2] Performativity is not like playing a dramatic role on the stage:

> Performativity is not a decision that one makes, nor is it a discrete or singular act.... It is a reiteration that is *not* chosen or performed by a subject that pre-exists the performance; instead, it is the constraint and regularization that forms one as a subject. (2001, 96, emphasis in original)

We enact the thoughts and emotions of sex and gender according to the norms and standards of proper performance. This chapter looks at the proper performance of emotional expression by women and men.

Once we understand that such culturally prescribed performances involve embodied habits that constitute our very will and self-identity, we can see why "gender is not something to be donned and discarded at will" (Sullivan 2001, 96). This does not mean our embodying of gender is forever bound to obey the commands of culture. Sullivan's transactionalism not only grasps the part of the discursive body "in which conceptions are constitutive of that which is conceived," but also the fact that "bodies that are discursively constituted are also actively constitutive of the political and other discourses that constitute them" (57). The same habits that constrain and coerce also enable and empower free agency. Dewey reminds us, "Habit is however more than a restriction of thought. Habits become negative limits because they are first positive agencies" (MW 14: 123). Further, because habits are plastic, they are subject to reconstruction.

Many things, including parents, peers, and the popular media, seize us before we critically comprehend them. Dewey distinguishes "individual minds" from "individuals with minds" (LW 1: 169). Only the former have minds of their own apart from the minds customarily found in their culture. "Individuals minds" have passed through a process of cultural critique, personal reflection, and self-creation. If people are ever to possess "selves" and realize their own unique potential, then they must analyze and reconstruct their cultural context. That is the function of intelligence in the quest for freedom, including emotional freedom.

Dewey's Theory of Emotions

Dewey published two coupled papers on the theory of emotions in the mid-1890s. The theory is, however, remarkably compatible with contemporary empirical studies. I do not have the space to get into any of the details of that theory here, though I have done so elsewhere.[3] For our purposes, the distinction between being in an affective state (raw feeling) and having an emotion is crucial. For Dewey, all emotions are cognitive, that is, they have a teleological object toward which the agent directs their activity. Even pathological emotions have such objects, though they may be the product of delusional interpretation or perhaps psychotropic drugs. Physiologically, noncognitive affective states (undefined feelings) are due to the autonomic nervous system (ANS) associated with the lower cortical sensory thalamus and amygdala. Cognitive states include the ANS but involve processing via higher brain functions, including the prefrontal cortex, among many other things. The higher sensory cortex permits the construction of a noetic object that directs the emotional reactions of the agent.

Unlike vague, indeterminate, floating feelings, emotions are cognitive because they are under the control of a habit or habit cluster that shapes actions and scripts performances in response to specific situations, objects, and, especially important to us, other people. It is important to recognize that we experience anoetic feelings. In an important sense, we have and are such affective states, but in themselves they are meaningless, unnameable, and unknowable. They possess us, but we do not necessarily possess them, even when we are consciously aware of them. Such conscious awareness, however, at least provides the possibility of further intelligent functioning that may render the feeling under our cognitive control. Even when feelings become meaningful, nameable, and knowable emotions, they may still control us rather than us controlling them. That means we are not yet free of our own needs, desires, and such. It is here that intelligence may enable freedom.

For Dewey, thought and feeling are functionally coordinated within the unity of the acts that habits help coordinate:

> We are easily brought to the conclusion that *the mode of behavior is the primary thing, and that the idea and the emotional excitation are constituted at one and the same time; that, indeed, they represent the tension of stimulus and response within the coordination which makes up the mode of behavior.* (EW 4: 174, emphasis in original)

In Dewey's theory, cognition and affect are phases or subfunctions within a single functional coordination. Affect and cognition emerge and clarify themselves as phases within the larger durational-extensional process of the individual body-mind's efforts to functionally coordinate its behavior. The pattern of functional coordination here is the same as that between stimulus and response in Dewey's famous reflex paper that appeared a year latter. For Dewey, we cannot unify our action until thought coordinates with feeling, though during any phase of the process of coordination one might temporarily prove more important than the other. Habits connect and control thinking, feeling, and acting.

When in either a noetic or an anoetic affective state, the ANS system is functioning. Many things accompany ANS arousal. For instance, activation of the system may accelerate heart rate, tear glands, bladder, stomach secretion, eye dilation, the muscles in the face, and so on. Being in such states does not constitute an emotional expression. They are simply neurophysiological states that are not, initially, under our control. That is, they are not intentional emotional expressions such as an actor on the stage may learn to emit. This fact leads to much confusion that we will need to clear up.

Ekman has established the existence of complex, coordinated, and automatic "affect program" responses. (1998, Afterword).[4] These programs centralize themselves in the older part of the cortex involving especially the amygdala and lower brain stem functions. They resemble reflexes, only they are more complexly coordinated. Ekman has established the existence of universal, genetically inherited affect programs that are independent of environmental influence, and he offers compelling evidence of pancultural agreement regarding the interpretation of what he calls "emotional expressions" that he thinks are also innate.

Initially, for Dewey, the gestures, tears, and laughter accompanying ANS arousal are simply acts, not expressions of significant meanings.[5] Upon reflective inquiry, however, an observer, or the individual themselves, may identify the act as expressive. Facial configurations only become meaningfully communicative gestures for those who know how to interpret them as signs expressing the emotional state of the body-mind displaying them. Likewise, those who are able to take the attitude of the other may intentionally express emotions (including deliberately misleading expressions). Dewey uses the phrase "the psychologist's fallacy" to describe what happens when we "confuse the standpoint of the observer and explainer with that of the fact observed" (EW 4: 154). Ekman's argument for innate emotions commits this fallacy, though he is correct that there are innate "affect program" responses.[6]

Communicative functions, including emotional expression, may *emerge* from our affective ANS states, but they are not primordial. Socialization includes learning the norms of where and how to express our emotions so others may respond to us appropriately.[7] All activity (movement, behavior, etc.) is meaningless in itself. Meanings, including meaningful emotional expressions, emerge from physical and biological activity without breach of continuity. Others realize the linguistic potential of our behavioral movements such as facial gestures, tears, and so on when they *interpret* them (rightly or wrongly) as gestures having specific consequences. For someone who knows how to interpret the signs, a body-mind may communicate thoughts and emotions even when that is not the intent. If when we are playing poker, I draw a card, suddenly bet everything I have, and my eyes dilate, it does not mean I intend to communicate to you that I have an unbeatable hand. If you know how to interpret the signs correctly, however, I may nonetheless communicate something I would rather conceal. Almost everyone in any culture will learn to read facial configurations if they learn to coordinate their social transactions at all well. That means they must *learn* to interpret the affective ANS gestures of others. Since we inherit some of these facial configurations, it is not surprising that the interpretation of some emotions, such as anger and fear, is pancultural. Ekman's affect program responses are actually only an important part, a subfunction, of emotional activity that shows that there are innate tendencies toward certain motor responses.

In spite of the fact that affect program responses are innate, emotions vary across cultures in ways, I want to suggest, that also vary across genders. The Japanese, for instance, experience an emotion called *amae* that involves a gratifying sense of being dependent on another person or organization, which is not usually found among Westerners. Westerners with no experience with Japanese culture are rarely able to read the facial expressions of *amae*, even when the subject is trying with conscious intent to communicate the emotion.

Ekman carried out cross-cultural research comparing Japanese and American college students.[8] Subjects from each culture were split into two groups; one group watched a stress-inducing film, while the other watched a neutral travelogue. Researchers videotaped the facial expressions of individuals subjected to both treatments. American students had no trouble deciding whether the Japanese students were watching a stressful or nonstressful film from examining the videotapes; the converse also held for the Japanese students examining videotapes of the Americans. These results held with very high correlations while the students reported their judgments when alone. A cultural difference, though, was identified. Here is how Ekman describes it:

> But when there was another person present the Japanese and Americans, as predicted, showed entirely different facial expressions. The Japanese showed more smiling than the Americans to mask their negative emotional expression. No wonder that foreigners, travelers and anthropologists who visited or lived among the Japanese thought their expressions different from Americans. (1998, 385)

Japanese subjects cut off short the expression of negative emotions in response to stressful stimuli if they experience the stimuli in the presence of outsiders, authority figures, or strangers. Ekman takes such examples as instances of socioculturally mediated "display rules" that override or mask affect response programs (1998, 384). Cultural display rules are embodied in cultural meanings whose interpretants are generalized *norms* of action called "habits."

The following passage from Dewey is not a direct statement about emotions, emotional meaning, or the cultural construction of emotions, but it is easy to convert it into one. All we have to do is substitute emotional meanings for "meanings," "making a face" for hand movement or "whistle," and "display rules" for "rules":

Meanings are objective because they are modes of natural interaction....A regulative force of legal meanings affords a convenient illustration. A traffic policeman holds up his hand or blows
a whistle....It embodies a rule of social action. Its proximate
meaning is its nearby consequences in coordination of movements of persons and vehicles; its ulterior and permanent meaning—essence—is its consequence in the way of security of social
movements....Its essence is the rule, comprehensive and per-
sisting, the standardized habit, of social interaction . . . . This
meaning is independent of the psychical landscape. (LW 1: 149)

Norms and standards of social action (e.g., cultural customs)
operating as emotional display rules may inscribe themselves as
habits on the body-minds of individuals as well as the body
politic to constrain and shape emotional behavior (expression,
interpretation, and response). Dewey's political socialism arises
from his social constructivist theory of mind and self.

Reflection on Western culture should allow us to readily
recognize how emotional display rules vary according to class,
race, gender, and so on. Some feminists for instance, have
already called attention to gender differences regarding such
display rules. Generally, girls learn they are allowed to display a
wider range of emotions, display more intense emotions, display
them more frequently, and display them in public. Meanwhile,
boys are taught rules that counter any kind of emotional expression at all (with one devastating exception), especially in public.
As adults, women and men in Western culture usually embody
different habits of emotional expression. As feminists have
shown, the dualism that constructs women as emotional and
men as rational is a hierarchy that insists reason should govern
emotion. The supposedly "natural" conclusion is that rational
men should govern emotional women.[9]

The Politics of Emotional Expression

If emotions are socially constructed, then they are bound to
have a politics. For instance, Haddock Seigfried shows in her
chapter how many of the women Jane Addams worked with
brought subtle, unconscious feelings of prejudice with them;

often these prejudices are far from subtle or unconscious. A politics of emotions should explore not only emotional expression but also the context wherein they occur, along with the interpretations and responses of others.[10] Power to enforce the rules lies behind the authority of the policemen. Power is not hard to understand; it is action taken for or against the possibility of action within a larger social transaction. Feminists argue that subtle systems of power shape the dominant emotional display rules in oppressive ways.[11] Judith Green indicates that for all his advantages, Dewey failed to provide an adequate account of "power structured relational differences like gender, race, culture, and class" (1999, 31).

Haddock Seigfried reconstructs Dewey to develop her version of pragmatist feminism. In a section in her book titled "Experience Is Emotional," she notes that emotions are public, not private, for Dewey. In spite of the quality of his insight into emotional experience, she nonetheless remarks that Dewey fails to analyze the "dark side" of experience. (1996, 168). For instance, she makes the following observation: "Enraged men do not always, or even often, pick a victim at random. Even random attacks on strangers are often selected in advance as to sex, race, and perceived vulnerability, if nothing else" (ibid.). Anger is the one emotion society permits males to display in public; sadly, Haddock Seigfried correctly states one of the widely circulating masculine emotional display rules. An adequate theory of the social construction of emotions, emotional communication, and emotional expression offers rich possibilities.

The following vignette of a dialogue across gender differences I once witnessed seems to require us to analyze the "dark side" of the social construction of emotional meaning. The vignette involves a new female teacher and a male administrator who called a meeting in which he promised the faculty could say whatever they felt needed saying for the purposes of reforming departmental programs. The teacher felt the need to express sympathetic concern for students caught in a certain institutional bind that the teachers in the program could ameliorate if they were willing to do a bit more work with students in advance of the start of classes. After the meeting, the senior teachers in the affected program complained to the administrator who called the young teacher into his office and accused her of being uncollegial. Other teachers outside of the program construed her concern for the students as being thoughtful and considerate not only of the students, but of her colleagues as well. In my opinion, they were correct. Further, again in my opinion, the teachers who complained were merely defending their authority in the existing faculty hierarchy while avoiding their responsibility to the students. In scolding the new teacher, the administrator chose to defend the status quo and annul his promise, which no one can guarantee anyway, that the meeting constituted a safe environment in which to express opinions. In conferring with the junior teacher later, she indicated to me that the administrator treated her paternalistically by acting condescending, dismissing her ideas along with her feelings of sympathy, and humiliating her by requiring she apologize to the offended senior teachers.[12] She maintained he would not have addressed her or the situation the same way had she been a male. The vicissitudes of human intention are notorious; it is the stuff of comedy and tragedy. What really happened? It depends on who tells the story and how one interprets it, interpretation, of course, being dependent on the individual's culturally inculcated habits.

Sue Campbell provides an interesting interpretive framework that suggests the possibility of gender bias in the foregoing vignette. In summing up her stance, Campbell makes three assertions that accord well with Dewey's, Mead's, and Sullivan's theories of the creation of meaning, mind, and the self, outlined earlier. First, she finds that "expression of feeling has an important public role" (1994, 54). Second, "The articulation of significance is possible, and only possible, through the use of such socially acquired resources as language, acting, and gesture, and various feelings may involve all or any of these" (ibid.). Finally, there is the "importance of locating the role of feelings as the attempt to articulate, form, or individuate a certain kind of *meaning* or *significance* in that such an account requires that our expressions of feeling be interpretable" (ibid., emphasis in original). Making audible expressions of emotion interpretable to others requires the one wishing to express her or his emotions

to have "an adequate range of resources to make the significance of things clear" to others while they provide "uptake" and
properly interpret the signs proffered (ibid.). Others provide
uptake when they take and use our gesture in the manner we
intended; that is, they interpret our acts as we would expect.

For pragmatists, interpretation requires participants to
come to an agreement about potential consequences. Making
our expressions interpretable to others involves taking their
attitude toward our own verbal gestures and other bodily signs.
The vicious irony is that those who have their emotions dismissed, and perhaps redesignated, in certain conversations, and
here I am thinking particularly about the discourses of power,
may never have the chance to acquire the requisite range of
resources required to make themselves clear. While hard to
detect, this is perhaps the most vicious and effective form of
oppressive power, since it allows the excluded other to internal-
ize not only thoughts but also feelings and images of her or his
own incapacity.

Campbell questions what happens when others refuse to
provide "uptake" (recognition, acknowledgment, etc.) of someone's emotions or redesignates them as something other than
what was intended. In the vignette just discussed, those in
power dismissed the teachers intended emotions of care and
compassion for students and redesignated them as arrogance
and, in the words of the new teacher, "bitchiness." In fact,
being called a "crazy bitch" is Campbell's first example of a
woman's emotion being dismissed and redesignated by other
participants in the transaction. Campbell concentrates on the
same emotion Haddock Seigfried calls attention to (i.e., emotions of anger) as well as bitterness (as the refusal to forgive
and forget) and sentimentality. These emotions are frequently
dismissed, though sometimes, as in the case of compassion,
they are simply devalued as a "virtue of femininity," which is a
vice in men.

Those who have the social power to refuse to listen, dismiss,
or interpretatively redesignate another's emotional expression
hold tremendous power. Indeed, the teacher I spoke with in the
earlier example felt helpless to protest or engage in further
action because she felt it might endanger her employment,

given where she was in the hierarchy. Since meaning is a social construction, such incidents may lead one to doubt one's own intentions. Many learn helplessness from such experiences of dismissal and redesignation.

We must, as Campbell puts it, comprehend "the power of interpreters to help determine [how] the situation may render our intentions unrecoverable and opaque," even to ourselves (1994, 49).[13] It is possible to exercise this power without conscious intent. Sometimes others simply do not embody the appropriate interpretants. The effect, however, is much the same whether intentional or not. We cannot see ourselves directly; others, with their habits of interpretation, must serve, at first, as the mirrors into which we look to understand our own emotions, thoughts, and actions. When the attitude of others is dismissive, we may become confused and begin to doubt our own thoughts and feelings. As the teacher, described earlier, searched to better understand her situation, she did express worry to me that she was being, in fact, uncollegial. We must remember that all mirrors distort the objects they reflect. In addition, we must learn to look as far inward as we do outward; conversely, I do think this teacher would have been helped if she could have taken an "observer theory" stance, as described by Reich and Neubert in their chapters.

Even when we are confident of the emotion we intend to express acoustically and otherwise, how others interpret our gestures or utterances, or their refusal to even listen, may hold power over us. For example, Campbell indicates "a certain mode of expression (recounting of injury) with a certain mode of response (failure to listen) forms bitterness" (1994, 51). It is a contingent, socially constructed attitude. Expanding on this theme, she observes that placing responsibility on the one expressing the emotion to communicate allows the recipient to evade her or his responsibility to recognize and respond to what the other is saying. The meanings constructed between speaker and hearer yield ugly consequences when systematically distorted by the interests of oppressive power.

Campbell observes that those "no longer caring to listen" can call on various forms of a socially accepted critique that then "becomes a reason or excuse for not listening" to another's expression (ibid.). She cites from Audre Lorde, who writes,

> I speak out of direct and particular anger at an academic conference, and a white woman says, "Tell me how you feel but don't say it too harshly or I cannot hear you." But is it my manner that keeps her from hearing, or the threat of a message that her life may change? (1994, 51)

Here the customary middle-class social norm of speaking in a calm and congenial way, and perhaps smiling often, becomes an excuse for not having to listen compassionately to the suffering, and perhaps bitterness and anger, of another. I have often seen expressions of suffering dismissed at academic conferences by the avatars of rational and critical thinking. Always insisting others "reason" as we do makes it easy to not listen to those who think differently, just as always doubting what others are trying to express is one way of protecting our present identity.

The woman Lorde describes in the previous quote, who felt threatened by a message that could change her life (by bringing feelings of guilt and perhaps a call to ameliorative action), understands that being a recipient of a communication that challenges one's habits of interpretation can alter one's identity. Believe me, I know the uncomfortable feeling of guilt; engendered discourse habits are excruciatingly hard to break. Still, the better emotion is the desire to alter one's conduct in the future by striving to build better relations today.

If the bodying of sex, much less gender, is contingent upon social constructions, then body-minds may become sexed and gendered through complex social transactions, as Sullivan clearly shows (2001, chap. 4). The question is *not* how I exercise my innate free will and rationality to reconstruct my habits of stylized gender performativity—such a question assumes a dualism that Dewey denies, which is that will and rationality somehow exist apart from the body in a special, preformed, psychic place called "mind." For Dewey, habits *are* will. It is not even quite right to ask how I can reconstruct my existing habits (how I can reconstruct my will) to free myself. For Dewey, habits *are* social. That means the reconstruction of existing habits is also social, which does not mean that it is entirely under social control.

Because we are body-minds whose gendered performative styles obey emotional display rules conditioned by entrenched cultural customs, the question is always: How can we contribute to self and society transactions that reconstruct both our body-minds and the body politic? Sullivan astutely observes:

> Dewey's notion of the plasticity of the self begins to answer the question concerning the circle between individual habit and cultural construct. What is frequently emphasized in the relationship between self and society is solely the society's ability to mold the self. What often is overlooked is the reciprocal ability of the self to transform its environment. (2001, 95)[14]

Those who succeed in becoming "individual minds" and not just individuals with minds may transform society in their future transactions with it. To become uniquely individual minds we must intelligently engage in transactions with contexts and people different from those who originally conditioned our habits of conduct. Participating in novel contexts with people whose bodying is different from our own releases novel impulses for action, creates new objects of desire, and allows us to alter our habitual plans of action.

Creative Intelligence and Emotional Freedom

For Dewey, "Intelligence is the key to freedom in act" (MW 14: 210). Until we become reflectively aware of our feelings, thoughts, and actions and inquire into their sources and destinations, they control and dominate us instead of us controlling them. I am interested in emotional freedom, so I will not deal with anoetic feelings except to acknowledge and respect them as always potentially communicable, hence, potentially meaningful, knowable, and controllable. Instead, I concentrate on affect as it appears under the control of noetic habits. I am especially interested in the formation of habits of emotional expression through participation in social transactions and what intelligent inquiry may contribute to emotional freedom.

We sustain freedom and growth through intelligent and creative action within our environment, especially our social environment, and not by some mysterious exercise of metaphysical freedom of will. For Dewey, freedom comprises: (1) "efficacy in action, [the] ability to carry out plans," (2) the "capacity to vary plans... to experience novelties," and (3) freedom "signifies the power of desire and choice to be factors in events" (LW 14: 209). For Dewey, choice is deliberate desire for what is within our power.[15] It is precisely here, though, that we can locate a serious omission in Dewey's notion of freedom; it sometimes omits the importance of material conditions. In *A Room of One's Own*, Virginia Woolf writes: "Intellectual freedom depends on material things" (1929, 108). Woolf thought that for a woman to be creative, she needed economic security and privacy; the same holds for anyone, of course, but those who have both in abundance are unlikely to mention either of them as conditions of freedom. Intelligence requires material support and room to operate.

The term *intelligence* derives from the Latin *inter* (between) and *legere* (among). It includes an astute use of affectively influenced selective interest and the release of novel impulse. It also includes not only the ability to choose wisely among alternatives, but to create new alternatives so that the false choices dictated to us by the dominate discourse do not enslave us. For Dewey, imagination is important to intelligent reflection. "Deliberation is a dramatic rehearsal (in imagination) of various competing possible lines of action" (LW 14: 132). Poetic creation constructs the path to wisdom. Intelligent deliberation involving unique individuals in diverse contexts is the key to freedom of choice. Such deliberation is embodied, impassioned, imaginative, and active as well as cognitive. In what follows, we will find that the pluralistic, democratic community is also an important part of the dialectic of freedom.

Dewey was aware that freedom originates not in consulting the natural light of reason or exercising metaphysical free will. We feel the first flickers of freedom before we think or know them. We must engage creatively in concrete action that transforms our thoughts and emotions. Reconstructing gender performativity is one such instance of transformation. Sullivan

follows Butler's notion of "bodily excess" in performativity as a
font of freedom. She reminds me of William Blake's pro-
nouncement: "The road of excess leads to the palace of
wisdom."[16] Wisdom refers to the truly good in action and,
hence, it always lies beyond knowledge alone, and especially
"knowledge" and the "good" as defined by those cultural norms
that oppress.

Sullivan critiques Butler's two primary strategies for reconstructing sedimented gender constructions by exploiting bodily
excess. Butler argues that we never incorporate a cultural norm
such as emotional display rules so perfectly that there is no
room for change. No two bodies are genetically identical, and
no two body-minds have the same experiences. We all follow
cultural rules according to our uniquely embodied interpretation. Sullivan agrees with all of this as far as it goes. Still, she
worries, that "does not yet explain how a body exceeds the *social
norms* that form it, including its tones, gestures, and postures"
(2001, 100). Here we are interested in emotional tones, gestures, and postures. Sullivan suggests that a better "way of reading bodily excess would be to understand it as what Dewey calls
impulses" (101). It is a very good idea.

For Dewey, "Impulses are the pivots upon which the reorganization of activities turn; they are agencies of deviation,
for giving new directions to old habits and changing their quality" (MW 14: 67). Because impulses are in themselves indeterminate potentials, "Impulse is a source, an indispensable source,
of liberation; but only as it is employed in giving habits perti-
nence and freshness does it liberate power" (MW 14: 75).
Dewey saw this liberation as a part of "learning or educative
growth. Rigid custom signifies not that there are no such
impulses but that they are not organically taken advantage of"
(MW 14: 73).[17] It is not that the impulses exist separately from
the habit; instead, as Sullivan states, "Habit *is* the organization
of impulses themselves" (2001, 101 emphasis in original). When
we alter habits of conduct even slightly, there is always an excess
of impulses requiring reorganization.

When we indulge such impulses, we may experience what
Alison M. Jagger calls "outlaw emotions." When we display
such emotions, we cease being good little girls and boys. Jagger

remarks: "Outlaw emotions may be politically because episte-mologically subversive.... Outlaw emotions are distinguished by their incompatibility with the dominant perceptions and values" (1989, 160). Intelligent libratory teaching practices would actually allow students to sometimes break the rules so that they might experience their outlaw emotions. Pluralistic democracies provide just such possibilities. The point, then, is not to free ourselves from all impulses and habits that we may return to our prediscursive bodies and see others and ourselves as we all "truly" are. Instead, the goal is to examine our histori-cally inherited and unreflectively held habits while becoming consciously aware of the sociocultural practices that condi-tioned them.

Intelligent freedom for Dewey not only involves impulsive bodily action and intense imagination, it also provided a means for effectively integrating passions once released. Dewey stated:

> The conclusion is not that the emotional, passionate phase of action can be or should be eliminated in behalf of a bloodless reason. More "passions," not fewer, is the answer.... Reason... signifies the happy cooperation of a multitude of disposi-tions.... The man who would intelligently cultivate intelligence will widen, not narrow, his life of strong impulses while aiming at their happy coincidence. (MW 14: 136–37)

Dewey embraces Rousseau's recognition that only passions can contrapuntally harmonize other passions. For Dewey, we embody intelligence and rationality, and they involve desire and even innate impulses. Dewey's view of intelligence conflicts with modernity's notion of transcendent a priori reason. Dewey wrote, "'Reason' is not an antecedent force.... It is a laborious achievement of habit needing to be continually worked over" (MW 14: 137). Dewey's goal is to free intelligence to grow by creatively reconstructing it and its world.

This brings us to Sullivan's comments on Butler's second suggestion as to how we may break through encrusted social norms by following the road of bodily excess to the palace of wisdom. Butler accurately calls attention to the fact that when we rely on habitual conduct in contexts other than those wherein the habit was originally conditioned, the consequences often confound action rather than coordinate it. Sullivan reminds us that for Dewey, "Education instead means helping the young form the habit of questioning, rethinking, and rebodying their own and their cultures' gender habits" (Sullivan 2001, 104). We can acquire the intelligent habit of reflecting on our own habits as well as the customs of the culture that originally conditioned those habits. We can acquire the habit of recreating our habits. Participating in many different contexts of practice, including reading unfamiliar texts, aids in this process considerably. While even the most totalizing of totalitarian cultures has some internal diversity, pluralistic democracy is far more intelligent in its ability to harness diversity for the good of the whole. In his chapter, "Creative Democracy—The Task before Us," Dewey declares:

> To cooperate by giving differences a chance to show themselves because of the belief that the expression of difference is not only a right of other persons but is a means of enriching one's own life-experience, is inherent in the democratic personal way of life. (LW 14: 228)

A pluralistic democracy provides many different contexts for carrying out conduct with those different from ourselves that are sure to challenge sedimented habits of personal identity and will. Green indicates that "Dewey's ideal of *deep democracy* necessarily implies *deep continuing diversity*" (1999, 59 emphasis in original). Intelligent pluralistic democracies manage diversity to eliminate what Green calls "*harmful difference-creating structures*" that divide and oppress while accentuating those that "cannot and should not be eliminated," because they allow us to remain open to the creative possibility necessary to survive in a complex, ever-evolving, Darwinian world.

What matters is not diversity per se but the transformations that arise because of diverse transactions. Dewey is especially interested in the transformations that emerge in communicative transactions. He affirms that, for logic, "The final actuality is accomplished in face-to-face relationships by means of direct give and take. Logic in its fulfillment recurs to the primitive sense of the word: *dialogue*. Ideas which are not communicated, shared, and reborn in expression are but [monological] soliloquy, and soliloquy is but broken and imperfect thought" (LW 2: 371, emphasis in original). Dewey's etymology here is correct. The term *logos* derives from the Greek "speech" or "word." For Dewey, democracy was the most logical form of government because it sought to facilitate communication. Further, he asserted that democracy was the best way to pursue logic. Dewey believes that "*Logic is a social discipline*," and that we are "*naturally* a being that lives in association with others in communities possessing language, and, therefore, enjoying a transmitted culture. Inquiry is a mode of activity that is socially conditioned and that has cultural consequences" (LW 12: 26–27, emphases in original). Intelligence lies in many places, including creative imagination, liberated impulses, and, of course, the living *logos*.[18] When we add new voices to a conversation, we also add interpretations that reconstruct the conditions of inquiry, including potentially the canons of rationality and the norms of action, including emotional display rules.[19]

Initially, we are not even aware of the cultural customs that prescribe habits of conduct such as emotional display rules. If we cannot consciously identify the habits that constitute our identities, then in some sense we do know ourselves; we are merely individuals with minds. That is precisely why differences are essential to achieving new understandings. Not until we encounter the differences poised by another's thoughts, emotions, and actions can we recognize our own habits and prejudices, much less inquire about them. We can know ourselves only if we know others different from ourselves, and others different from ourselves only if we know ourselves. Transacting with unique persons in novel contexts contributes to our capacity to transgress sedimented cultural norms such as engendered rules of emotional display. Those who are different from us enact the drama of their lives using a different vocabulary, a different grammar, different plot lines, and different tropes, and they express a different style. That is why pluralistic democracy is the best, most intelligent form of community.

Conclusion: Pluralistic Communicative
Democracy, Diversity, and Growth

Let us recognize the attractiveness of totalitarian thought and totalitarian political regimes. They allow us to avoid novel contexts and unique individuals that challenge our identity. Totalitarianism brings self-satisfied contentment. It arises from the realization that novel contexts may contain poison, and strange people may slay us. Therein lies the power that totalitarians will always have over us.

Pluralism, including pluralistic communicative democracy, not only brings discomfort but genuine danger. To live we must eat, drink, and breath, which renders us open and vulnerable, thereby rendering total isolation impossible. Besides, in a Darwinian universe, isolation is usually the greater danger. Still, Dewey admits

> No adult environment is all of one piece. The more pluralist a culture, the more likely its members will possess conflicting habits. Each custom may be rigid, unintelligent in itself, and yet this rigidity may release impulse for new adventure.... Different institutions foster antagonistic impulses and form contrary dispositions. (LW 14: 90)

Democratic diversity is not for our comfort; being for our growth, it is for our pruning. Dewey further insists, "Any self is capable of including within itself a number of inconsistent selves, of unharmonized dispositions" (LW 14: 96). Already, even at the level of unconscious impulse and habit, we are always in a dialogue across difference "within" ourselves.

The pluralistic nature of the self provides perhaps the most hidden possibility of openness to transgression of norms and transformation of self and world. Bruce Wilshire asserts that, for Dewey, the "subconscious means and meanings do not form a coherent system. Dewey's exhibition of this devastates any optimistic view of the human condition. He thinks the 'soul of modern man' is a hellish mess.... T[hat] should forever dispel the illusion of the kindly, grandfatherly, benign, and optimistic

Dewey" (1993, 267). There is another way to respond to such inner diversity. Dewey embraced Emerson in many ways. I think he would have fully approved of the following passage from Emerson's essay "Self-Reliance": "A foolish consistency is the hobgoblin of little minds, adored by little statesmen and philosophers and divines. With consistency a great soul has simply nothing to do" (1926, 41).[20] The permanent possibility for dialogue across different sociocultural customs lives, among many other places, within the deep recesses of the unconsciousness mind.

Becoming aware of the tensions found in the dialogues across differences within ourselves could cause us to desire dialogues across differences outside of ourselves. Of course, conceived transactionally as a function distributed throughout a world without withins, the tensions seemingly within originated with our initiation into the cultural customs and social practices of the world seemingly without.[21] Freedom for Dewey is the holistic consequence of physical action, vivid imagination, disciplined desire, and diverse community.[22] Reflective intelligence allows us to become conscious of our thoughts, emotions, and actions as well as how our environment conditions them. For those who understand transactionalism and functional dependence, such knowledge allows them to reconstruct themselves by reconstructing the environment that initially conditioned their habits of conduct. What Neubert says about repeatedly having to construct, deconstruct, and reconstruct our methods with regard to the concrete problems and situations we have to deal with holds equally well for ourselves, for our personal identity.

Creative intelligence allows us to first carry out plans, imagine ideal alternatives to oppressive actual states of affairs, and then develop plans for bodying these valued objects of desire and choice. In "Self-Reliance," Emerson also writes: "To talk of reliance is a poor external way of speaking. Speak rather of that which relies because it works and is" (1926, 50). Creative intelligence may free us from constraint, but genuine freedom requires us to bind our body-minds to those persons, places, and things upon which we must rely because they are most conducive to our growth, and we to them.

Notes

1. Sullivan is fully aware that there is a meaningful, nonlinguistically lived sense of the body. She writes: "We can think of bodies as discursively constituted at the same time we can acknowledge the existence of and the powerful information provided by a felt bodily sense that is nonlinguistic" (2001, 52). We experience anoetic feelings; however, any emotion, any thought, and any intentional act directed toward the world, others, or ourselves is a noetic cultural construction. Self-knowledge requires becoming conscious of our feelings and thoughts and then reflectively realizing that any discursive meaning we may assign them involves cultural norms. Acquiring such self-knowledge is crucial to Dewey's concept of freedom.

2. Sullivan remarks, "To be a 'real' woman in Western culture has meant and, to a considerable extent, still means to comport oneself in a generally deferential, nonconfrontational, and passive manner: smiling, 'containing one's bodying so that it occupies minimal physical space, and so on" (2001, 105). She then contrasts these "virtues" with the confrontational, aggressive, "masculine" performativity characteristic of "real" philosophers.

3. See Garrison (2003).

4. This paragraph and the five that follow it rely extensively on Garrison (2003).

5. Dewey states:

> There is no such thing (from the standpoint of the one having the experience) as expression. We call it expression when looking at it from the standpoint of an observer.... The very word "expression" names the facts not as they are, but in their second intention. To an onlooker my angry movements are expressions— sign, indications; but surely not to me. To rate such movements as primarily expressive is to fall into the psychologist's fallacy: it is to confuse the standpoint of the observer and explainer with that of the fact observed. Movements *are*, as a matter of fact, expressive, but they are also a great many other things. In themselves they are movements, acts. (LW 3: 154)

6. We do not learn how to be afraid, that is innate, but we do need to learn what to be afraid of (the teleological object around which we coordinate our transactions).

7. Dewey remarks that his position is "in no way inconsistent with the development of certain movements to serve as expressive. On the contrary, since movements take place in a social medium, and their recognition and interpretation by others is a fact of positive import in the struggle for existence, we might expect the development of gesture and signs through selection" (EW 4: 154).

8. See Ekman (1972, 207–83).

9. Dewey explicitly denies the dualism between emotion and reason; consider the following:

> The conclusion is not that the emotional, passionate phase of action can be or should be eliminated in behalf of a bloodless reason. More "passions," not fewer, is the answer. . . . rationality, once more, is not a force to evoke against impulse and habit. It is the attainment of a working harmony among diverse desires. "Reason" as a noun signifies the happy cooperation of a multitude of dispositions. (MW 14: 136)

Passages such as this one are why pragmatist feminists find Dewey a good starting point for launching feminist critiques. Nonetheless, they rightly find Dewey requires considerable reconstruction.

10. Men often interpret attempted emotional expressions by women, especially anger, as hysteric, unfeminine, or "nutty," and they simply dismiss them. According to Campbell, when the interpretations and responses of others in our culture fail to validate our affective expression, women or men experience frustration, silencing, and oppression. For Dewey, meanings emerge in a transactional coordination among two or more emergent centers of linguistic transaction. In an especially Deweyan passage, Campbell concludes:

> [I]f someone consistently fails to secure uptake [acknowledgment] for their feelings that get formed only through acts of expression, it cannot be clear even to that person what she or he is feeling, and many peoples' emotional lives are, in fact, dominated by a confusion that is an inevitable consequence of persistent lack of uptake. (1994, 55)

Meanings, including the meanings of our emotional life, are contingent sociocultural constructions that depend on our transactions with others no matter one's gender, race, ethnicity, social class, sexual preference, and so on. The chapters by Hickman and Seigfried in this book help us see how meanings may evolve and perhaps even grow.

11. I believe these observations hold for Eastern as well as Western cultures.

12. I believe there were also power plays involving the junior faculty member and senior female members who are protecting their privilege. That the senior women were willing to invoke an administrative patriarch to preserve advantage is a sad irony.

13. For more on power and the social construction of the self from the perspective of Köln Interactive Constructivism, see the chapters by Reich and Neubert in this book. While Dewey is quite good when discussing power to, power for, and power with, he requires a stronger concept of oppressive power.

14. Sullivan cites the following passage from Dewey in which he asserts that the self "seems putty to be molded according to current designs. That plasticity also means power to change prevailing custom is [too often] ignored" (MW 14: 47).

15. The role of deliberation in choice for Dewey strongly resembles that of Aristotle, who characterizes choice in the *Nicomachean Ethics* as "thinking desire." Following Dewey, Sullivan recognizes that while structures such as habits can constrain us, hence we must often free ourselves *from* restraint, structures also provide the power *to* achieve goals, which often requires power *with* others in community. Sullivan calls attention to the follow passage:

> [T]here can be no greater mistake...than to treat freedom as an end in itself....For freedom from restriction, the negative side, is to be prized only as a means to a freedom which is power: power to frame purposes, to judge wisely, to evaluate desires by the consequences which will result from acting upon them; power to select and order means to carry chosen end into operation. (LW 13: 41)

While Dewey may not have fully comprehended oppressive power, he had an excellent understanding of power to, for, and with.

16. See the "Proverbs of Hell" in William Blake's ([1793] 1988) *The Marriage of Heaven and Hell.*

17. Earlier in this book, Reich and Neubert also made important connections among habits, impulses, and growth in the context of Dewey's essential criteria for describing the democratic community, cultural context, and individual selective interests. I would like to remind the reader of their discussions, since it adds a great deal to what I am trying to say here.

18. Dewey is committed to deliberative, communicative democracy, which is why he says it "is more than a form of government; it is primarily a mode of associated living, of conjoint communicated experience" (MW 9: 93).

19. Dewey also is committed to pluralistic democracy; see (MW 9: 93).

20. See also, "Emerson—The Philosopher of Democracy" (MW 3: 184–92). It is a "foolish consistency" that Dewey would decry, not the functional coordination of conduct through intelligent inquiry.

21. Reflecting on a long list of dualisms, Dewey remarks:

The material and spiritual, the physical and the mental or psychological; body and mind; experience and reason; sense and intellect, appetitive desire and will; subjective and objective, individual and social; inner and outer; this last division underlying in a way all the others. (LW 16: 408)

22. I explore these themes in detail in Garrison (1997).

Works Cited

Blake, W. [1793] 1988. The marriage of heaven and hell. In *The complete poetry and prose of William Blake*, ed David V. Endman, 33–45. New York: Doubleday.

Butler, J. 1990. *Gender trouble*. New York: Routledge.

———. 1993. *Bodies that matter: On the discursive limits of "sex."* New York: Routledge.

———. 1997. *Excitable speech: A politics of the performative*. New York: Routledge.

Campbell, S. 1994. Being dismissed: The politics of emotional expression. *Hypatia* 9: 3 46–65.

Ekman, P. 1972. Universals and cultural differences in facial expressions of emotion; In *Nebraska symposium on motivation, 1971*, ed. J. Cole, Lincoln: University of Nebraska Press.

———. 1998. Afterword. In *The expression of the emotions in man and animals*, ed. P. Ekman, 363–93. Oxford: Oxford University Press.

Emerson, R. W. [1841] 1926. Self-reliance." In *Essays by Ralph Waldo Emerson*. New York: Thomas Y. Crowell Company.

Garrison, J. 1997. *Dewey and eros: Wisdom and desire in the art of teaching*. New York: Teachers College Press.

———. 2003. Dewey's theory of emotions: The unity of thought and emotion in naturalistic functional "Coordination" of behavior. *Transactions of the Charles S. Peirce Society* 39:3 405–43.

Green, J. 1999. *Deep democracy: Community, diversity, and transformation*. New York: Rowman & Littlefield.

Jagger, A. M. 1989. Love and knowledge: Emotion in feminist epistemology. In *Gender/body/knowledge*, ed. Alison M. Jagger and Susan R. Bordo, 145–71. New Brunswick, NJ: Rutgers University Press.

Seigfried, C. H. 1996. *Pragmatism and feminism: Reweaving the social fabric*. Chicago: University of Chicago Press.

Sullivan, S. 2001. *Living across and through skins*. Bloomington: Indiana University Press.

Wilshire, B. 1993. Body-mind and subconsciousness: Tragedy in Dewey's life and work. In *Philosophy and the reconstruction of culture*, ed. John J. Stuhr, 257–72. Albany: State University of New York Press.

Woolf, V. 1929. *A room of one's own*. New York: Harcourt Brace & Co.

Chapter 8

Moral Norms and Social Inquiry

Hans Seigfried

Richard Rorty claims that "the attempt...to get 'ready-made rules available at a moment's notice for settling any kind of moral difficulty', seemed to Dewey to have been 'born of timidity and nourished by love of authoritative prestige'." Only such a tendency to sadomasochism, Dewey thought, could have led to the idea that 'absence of immutably fixed and universally applicable ready-made principles [like Kant's categorical imperative] is equivalent to moral chaos' " (Rorty 1999, 75; see also Dewey MW 14: 164). I want to discuss Dewey's efforts to carry over "the essential elements of the pattern of experimental knowing into the experience of man in its everyday traits," and I shall argue that the idea of operationally a priori principles is a more solid basis for social hope, and democracy, than the popular belief that the acceptance of fixed universal moral norms in all areas, especially in advanced research and technology, will help us solve the more serious conflicts that occur in life (LW 4: 155). In Part I, I discuss the idea of experimental-operational rules, axioms, and principles. There I pursue Dewey's remark that "principles treated as fixed rules instead of as helpful methods take men away from experience" (MW 14: 164). In the much shorter Part II, I review the use of these concepts in social inquiry, which serves to test them, as Dewey says.

Part I: Principles of Inquiry as Helpful Methods

Without the explicit formulation of guiding principles, inquiry in any field remains what Kant called "a merely random groping" (1965, BVII). Ordinarily, successful research strategies get preserved in institutions, but if their conceptual apparatus becomes habitual, or if it is inadequately formulated, then it defeats inquiry, as Dewey observes:

> Directing conceptions tend to be taken for granted after they have once come into general currency. In consequence they either remain implicit or unstated, or else are propositionally formulated in a way which is static instead of functional. Failure to examine the conceptual structures and frames of reference which are unconsciously implicated in even the seemingly most innocent factual inquiries is the greatest single defect that can be found in any field of inquiry. Even in physical matters, after a certain conceptual frame of reference has once become habitual, it tends to become finally obstructive with reference to new lines of investigation. (LW 12: 501)

In his 1938 *Logic: The Theory of Inquiry*, Dewey argues that in order to turn evolved strategies into operational rules, axioms, and principles that are necessary for programmed research, we need logical "legislation." I begin my discussion of this seemingly outlandish claim with a brief review of what Dewey describes as a common pattern of inquiry.

Dewey notes that we can distinguish five steps for completing a thought, that is, for establishing a proposition and "warrantably assertible conclusion," through controlled inquiry. Their sequence is not fixed, and they may vary in scope (MW 6: 236–41; see also LW 8: 200-209). His final account lists (1) a description of the existential conflict situation that calls for inquiry, (2) the institution of the problem, (3) the formulation of an idea of a solution, or end in view, (4) reasoning, namely, review of the relevance of connected ideas ("suggestions") and development of a "proposition" about what needs to be done, and (5) a review of available resources, namely, the establishment of facts relevant to the proposed solution (LW 12: 105–22). All of these operations are required for a warranted assertion about what needs and can be done to resolve an existing conflict; it is only on the basis of these combined operations that we can meaningfully expect to acquire the confidence in ideas that is required for warranted assertions and the decision to act on them.

It would be a mistake, it seems to me, to say that the end of inquiry is the resolution of existential conflict situations. It makes no sense to say that such a resolution is the end of inquiry as inquiry, that is, that it answers the question "What could be done to resolve the existential conflict?" The grounds for answering this question must be given in advance of action; once action has resolved the conflict, the question becomes redundant and meaningless. As Dewey points out, warranted assertions are "operational agencies by which *beliefs* that have adequate grounds for acceptance are reached as *end* of inquiry" (LW 14: 175, emphasis in original). Of course, the end of inquiry as an instrument for the transformation of existential conflict can only be the outcome of the action taken, that is, the question "Did the action, recommended by the warranted assertion, resolve the conflict?" can only be given in consequence of the action taken. Certainly a warranted assertion can be instrumental for taking action, that is, for getting the courage to take action, but it is not the result of the action taken.

In his short catechism concerning truth, Dewey contends that "experience is a matter of functions and habits, of active adjustments and readjustments, of coordinations and activities, rather than of states of consciousness" that mysteriously represent the real (MW 6: 5 ff.). It is the transformation of uncertain, disturbed existential situations by operations that modify existing conditions so they get integrated into harmonious situations. In the course of it, we draft ideas of means and ends and strategies for creating settled situations in which people can realize their capacities. These ideas are not representations of existing conditions but anticipations of consequences, forecasts of what does not yet exist anywhere, and therefore embodied in symbols. The ideas (including the idea of democracy) are then

---

Hans Seigfried

examined for their functional fitness for resolving existential conflict situations, and thus they become operational in that they instigate and direct further operations of observation; they are proposals and plans for acting upon existing conditions to bring new facts to light and to organize all of the selected facts into a coherent whole (LW 12: 116).

The observed facts, "which present themselves in consequences of the experimental observations the ideas call out and direct, are trial facts" that are as operational as are the ideas, because they are selected, described, and arranged for solving the conflict in a given situation, and because they are such that they fit together in ways adequate for that purpose. They are provisional facts, because they have yet to be tested for evidence "of their power to exercise the function of resolution" in the case, and it has yet to be demonstrated by experiment that they can be instrumental in the matter (117).

As long as the resolution remains a mere possibility, however, it can be worked out only in symbolic form, regardless of the actual status of the observed trial facts. For the resolution cannot be carried to term unless the trial facts are functionally connected to the conflict that calls for inquiry, and they can be so connected only with the help of ideas and symbols in propositions. Very unlike in traditional (representational) theories of inquiry, in Dewey's operational account propositions are proposals in which what is "pre-sented" in observation is tentatively projected onto the conflict that calls for inquiry and taken as "representative" for its resolution. Without such symbolic propositional connection, the observed facts would simply "relapse into the total qualitative situation" and lose their significance for the resolution of the conflict through inquiry. As Dewey points out in his final response to Russell's critique, propositions so understood "are means, instrumentalities, since they are operational agencies by which beliefs that have adequate grounds for acceptance [warranted assertions] are reached as end of inquiry" (LW 14: 175).

The symbolic propositional connections of particular operations, however, cannot be what Dewey has in mind with logical forms of inquiry. Propositional forms of themselves are not logical forms. Such propositional connections are means for attaining judgments, or warranted assertions, concerning a given problem; they are "operational agencies" for initiating the action required for the desired reshaping of antecedent existential subject matters or for the transformation of a given problematic into a resolved unified situation. Ordinarily we make such connections by following the tracks of successful past operations, cultivated habits, and established patterns. We are able to derive from such operations, habits, and patterns what Dewey calls "logical forms" only if we can experimentally establish what shapes, forms, and determines them, and then accept it as a rule, or set of rules, for further inquiry.

Any habit is a way or manner of action, not a particular act or deed. When it is formulated it becomes, as far as it is accepted, a rule, or more generally, a principle or "law" of action. It can hardly be denied that there are habits of inference, and they may be formulated as rules or principles. If there are such habits as are necessary to conduct every successful inferential inquiry, then the formulations that express them will be logical principles of all inquiries (LW 12: 21).

"Successful" simply means that in its continuity inquiry produces results that are either confirmed or corrected in further inquiry "by use of the same procedures," and by actions based on them. This sameness constitutes ways, habits, customs, and traditions of inquiry. But by themselves, such invariants are not principles, axioms, rules, and binding laws that can and must govern all inquiries. Only if they meet certain conditions capable of formal statement can we turn them into binding laws and recognize them as the logical forms of all inquiry, namely, demands that inquiry in the complete sense must satisfy. These conditions, and not the common traits of habits, customs, and traditions of inquiry, are, therefore, the proper subject matter of logical analysis, as Dewey argues in the opening chapter of his *Logic* (9–29). Since these conditions can be discovered in the course of inquiry itself, it is not necessary to assume that they somehow "subsist prior to and independently of inquiry," either as Platonic forms or as Kantian structures of consciousness that "are completely and inherently a priori and are disclosed to a faculty called pure reason" (LW 12: 23).

When we habitually use without formulation of a leading principle the same procedures that in the past yielded conclusions that were "stable and productive in further inquiry," our research efforts may be equally successful, in spite of differences of subject matter. Although Dewey claims at one point that when in a set of procedures habitually performed something invariant is noticed and made explicit in propositional form, then this formulation, "being free from connection with any particular subject-matter," becomes a leading formal principle for further research, it is obvious that being noticed and given propositional form cannot be enough for claiming it to be a binding rule for all inquiries; the propositional formulation of an invariant in relation to a specified set of procedures as such is not a logical form (LW 12: 20). The formulation becomes a logical form only when it is "accepted" as a rule or, more generally, as a principle or law of operations (21). The decisive condition, then, that a propositional form must satisfy in order to become a logical form of inquiry, is that it must be accepted and formally recognized as a binding rule for the operations of every successful inquiry, as defined earlier; logical legislation must impose on it the force of law.

In efforts to justify acts of logical legislation, it is tempting to misconstrue propositional forms that satisfy this condition as metaphysical presuppositions about experience or its existential material, or as premises of inference, in other words, to anchor them in some existential order which logical legislation merely makes explicit and to which it must conform in order to be justified. Dewey argues that such representational interpretations are unnecessary, because the rules of successful inquiry are to be understood as "directly operational" (9–29 passim). And as operational demands they obviously are conditions to be satisfied so that knowledge of them provides a principle of direction and of testing. They are ways of treating subject matter that have been found to be so determinative of sound conclusions in the past that they are taken to regulate further inquiry until definite grounds are found for questioning them. While they are derived from an examination of methods previously used in their connection to the kind of conclusion they have produced, they are operationally a priori with respect to further inquiry (21).

Against their epistemological and metaphysical interpretation, Dewey argues that as operational conditions imposed on future inquiries, logical forms must be "intrinsically postulates of and for inquiry"—*intrinsically*, because they must not be imposed from without but discovered in the course of inquiry itself, and *postulates*, because they can and must be nothing but stipulations and responsibilities accepted for the conduct of inquiry by those committed to it (23 ff.). He illustrates this point by comparing a law in the logical sense to a law in the legal sense, as follows:

> If anything has a certain property, and whatever has this property has a certain other property, then the thing in question has this certain other property. This logical "law" is a stipulation. If you are going to inquire in a way which meets the requirements of inquiry, you must proceed in a way which observes this rule, just as when you make a business contract there are certain conditions to be fulfilled and so on. (24)

The same must be said about the principles of identity, noncontradiction, excluded middle, the law of causality, the syllogistic forms, and so on.

According to the most notorious epistemological and metaphysical interpretations, on the other hand, the logical requirements of inquiry are "externally postulates" and "externally a priori" because they must be imposed from without, say from some fixed Platonic form that exists $K\alpha\theta$ $\alpha\nu\tau o$, or some fixed Kantian structure of consciousness, if inquiry is to yield warranted assertability as a consequence. But external requirements unavoidably obscure the conduct of controlled inquiry, because such fixed structures are, by definition, inaccessible to empirical inquiry and at odds with its continuity. Ironically, in Platonic and Kantian efforts to avoid arbitrariness and to secure unshakeable foundations for logical legislation, all is lost, because claims about such unchanging static external conditions can be maintained, Dewey argues, only on the basis of "an elaborate process of dialectic inference" (231). Kant's own efforts to secure "externally *a priori*" knowledge, so it seems, were as misled and unsuccessful as he scoldingly says Plato's were (1965, A5f./B9f.). They leave empirical inquiry without operational

guidance and direction and ignore the logical rules that continuously develop in inquiry itself.

But uneasiness with Dewey's idea of logical forms lately
bred interpretations that mean to show that his strictly operational a priori must be connected to, or anchored in, some independent metaphysical or ontological reality after all, or that the
necessity of logical forms must be different in kind from the
experimental necessity generated in inquiry, or that all propositions, including propositional formulations of the rules of
inquiry, must be interpreted in terms of classification or attribution, that is, that they are, or depend on, descriptions of generic
traits of existence (Sleeper 1986; Boisvert 1988; and others).

It would seem, however, that the interpretation of rules of
controlled inquiry as descriptions of realities or traits of realities
is deeply flawed, for reliable descriptions can be secured only
through the controlled operations of inquiry that bring out of
"the total qualitative situation" facts about realities that matter in
the resolution of existential conflicts that call for inquiry; propositions of classification and attribution are necessarily functions
of the propositional formulations of the rules that guide and
govern the controlled transactions of inquiry between environment, existential conflict situations, and their desired transformations. Without explicit formulation and acceptance of the
rules that govern such transactions, we would be left either with
the realities of as yet untested and thus haphazard transactions of
our ancestors, or with what William James notoriously called "a
big blooming buzzing confusion." The flaw, then, in the very
idea of realist or metaphysical interpretations of logical forms is
much more fatal than Dewey's observation, that "the interpretation of all propositions in terms of classification or attribution
(and of extension and intension) obscures their intermediary and
functional nature," suggests (LW 12: 298). For in order to be
able to claim that the propositional formulations of the rules of
inquiry must be based on descriptive propositions of realities,
one must be totally unaware of, or as Nietzsche argued, have
completely forgotten about, or deny altogether the "intermediary and functional nature" of such propositions (86 ff.).

The obvious source of the uneasiness with an operational
theory is the belief that it is much less capable of furnishing the
steady normative direction that is required for the control of

inquiry in the management of human affairs than "the classical type of logic."[1] Being strictly operational, logical forms are intrinsically limited postulates, and the more serious problems that occur in life, many believe, require universally applicable rules of inquiry that enable anyone to locate and solve such problems wherever and whenever they occur. We learn, however, from experimental scientists that what enables anyone to do so, ironically, are precisely the explicitly stated limited conditions, as Dewey observes:

> Postulates alter as methods of inquiry are perfected; the logical forms that express modern scientific inquiry are in many respects quite unlike those that formulated the procedures of Greek science. An experimenter in the laboratory who publishes his results states [1] the materials used, [2] the setup of apparatus and [3] the procedures employed. These specifications are limited postulates, demands and stipulations, for any inquirer who wishes to test the conclusion reached. Generalize this performance for procedures of inquiry as such, that is, with respect to the form of every inquiry, and logical forms as postulates are the outcome. (26)[2]

How, then, can we possibly hope to carry over "the essential elements of the pattern of experimental knowing into the experience of man in its everyday traits" and broaden it to insight into specific conditions of value and into specific consequences of ideas (LW 4: 155)? How can the plea for the limiting context of inquiry lead to the belief that the logical forms of modern inquiry must in time develop into "a method for locating and interpreting the more serious of the conflicts that occur in life, and a method of projecting ways for dealing with them: a method of moral and political diagnosis and prognosis" (MW 4: 13)? By using social inquiry "to test the general logical conceptions that have been reached," Dewey demonstrates at length how they can become such a method simply because information about the setup alone can tell inquirers what to look for and how to observe it, and thus participate in concerted efforts to address existing problems. Publishing results without detailed information about the setup would irresponsibly send others on a wasteful wild goose chase and turn controlled inquiry into "a merely random groping" (LW 12: 481–505).[3]

We have learned from modern physics that what reliable experimental observations we are able to make depends on the setup of apparatus in the narrow sense, as Dewey shows in his review of Heisenberg's principle of indeterminacy (LW 4: 160–64). But the lesson he draws from this fact is much broader, namely, that "knowing is one kind of interaction which goes on within the world," and "knowing marks the conversion of undirected changes into changes directed toward an intended conclusion" (163). This conclusion depends largely, though not exclusively, on the setup of the institutional "apparatus" that regulates research, namely, the logical forms that govern inquiry and determine the intricate organization of research programs with their specific fields, goals, commitments, assignments, tools, teams, and procedures.

Commenting on the broader consequences of the situation in modern physics, Dewey argues that it calls for a radical revision of the received concept of inquiry:

> If we persist in the traditional conception, according to which the thing to be known is something which exists prior to and wholly apart from the act of knowing, then discovery of the fact that the act of observation, necessary in existential knowing, modifies that preexistent something is proof that the act of knowing gets in its own way, frustrating its own intent.... Fundamentally, the issue is raised whether philosophy is willing to surrender a theory of mind and its organs of knowing which originated when the practice of knowing was in its infancy. (164)

Dewey's reconstruction avoids such frustration through the setup of laws of inquiry designed for prompting nature to release the resources required for the desired transformation of existential conflict situations that prompted the setup. This multiply corresponding setup sustains and guarantees the continuous transaction of inquiry.

Part II: Social Inquiry and Moral Norms as Conversation Stoppers

Dewey develops the principles of inquiry with the natural sciences in mind. In a broad sense of "natural," social sciences are branches of natural science, so one might assume that they follow the same principles, but the backwardness of social inquiry in comparison to physics and biology suggests that they might not. Could the same principles be used in social inquiry, and would their use improve the situation? To bar misunderstandings, Dewey insists that

> the question is not whether the subject-matter of human relations is or can ever become a science in the sense in which physics is now a science, but whether it is such as to permit the development of methods which, as far as they go, satisfy the logical conditions that have to be satisfied in [all] other branches of inquiry. That there are serious difficulties in the way is evidenced by the backward state of social inquiry. (LW 12: 481)

Given the sheer complexity of the field of human relations, it would seem unlikely that difficulties in the study of social matters could be resolved by satisfying the logical conditions of successful inquiry in all other fields. In "Social Inquiry," the longest chapter in his 1938 *Logic*, Dewey demonstrates how the more serious problems arise when some of the simple experimental-operational rules, axioms, and principles, made explicit in his theory, are ignored. I will review some such breaches and assess Dewey's handling of them in terms of philosophical promise and social hope.

The Special Status of Democratic Social Inquiry

Dewey claims that "all inquiry proceeds within a cultural matrix which is ultimately determined by the nature of social relations" (481). He defends this claim in the five chapters of Part One of *Logic*, "The Matrix of Inquiry." Although the search for "agreement of activities and their consequences" proceeds differently in different fields within this matrix, "the ultimate end and test of all inquiry is the transformation of a problematic situation (which involves confusion and conflict) into a unified [harmonious] one." The fact that such agreement is more difficult to achieve in social than in physical inquiry does not constitute "an inherent logical or theoretical difference between two kinds of inquiry" (484 ff.). So in order to be successful, the controlled

study of social relations must follow the same experimental
rules and principles, as do all other branches of inquiry with
existential subject matter.

People concerned with the democratic management of social
affairs and the funding of social research programs, Dewey
observes, commonly assume that "the problems which exist are
already definite in their main features. When this assumption is
made, it follows that the business of inquiry is but to ascertain
the best method of solving them" (487). Given this assumption,
along with the habit of "arguing toward the best solution," more
in vogue than ever, the controlled experimental observation and
analysis of social troubles required for converting them "into a
set of [objective] conditions forming a definite problem" is
skipped, and "the best solution" proposed remains "without any
clear conception of the [existing] material in which projects and
plans are to be applied and to take effect" (487).

Consequently, in order to be intelligently dealt with, social
troubles must be converted into definite problems, that is, they
must be methodically instituted on the basis of "controlled analytic observation" of existing conditions and their "objective
intellectual [conceptual] formulation, involving systematic comparison-contrast" (488).[4] This means that social inquiry must
resist the obstructive tendency to interpret serious social and
political troubles "in moral terms," because

> such a formulation demands in turn complete abstraction from
> the qualities of sin and righteousness, of vicious and virtuous
> motives, that are so readily attributed to individuals, groups,
> classes, nations.... Spinoza's contention that the occurrence of
> moral evils should be treated upon the same basis and plane as
> the occurrence of thunderstorms is justifiable on the ground of
> the requirements of scientific method.... For such procedure is
> the only way in which they can be formulated objectively or in
> terms of selected and ordered conditions. And such formulation
> is the sole mode of approach through which plans of remedial
> procedure can be projected in objective terms. Approach to
> human problems in terms of moral blame and moral
> approbation...is probably the greatest single obstacle now exist-
> ing to development of competent methods in the field of [social
> inquiry]. (LW 12: 488 ff.)

Facts, Values, and Moral Norms

The realization of "the harm that has been [done] by forming social judgments on the ground of moral preconceptions" has led others to assume, "in the professed name of social science," that

> the facts are out there and only need to be observed, assembled and arranged to give rise to suitable and grounded generalizations [and] that in order to base conclusions on the facts and only the facts, all evaluative procedures must be strictly ruled out. (489)

But this "scientific" approach to social troubles does even more harm than the moral approach. It not only stops social inquiry as definitively as the moral approach does, by adopting, as it were, T. H. Huxley's notorious recommendation for the study of nature, namely, "Sit down before the facts as a little child, be prepared to give up every preconceived notion, follow humbly wherever and to whatever abyss nature leads, or you shall learn nothing," but by completely ignoring the experimental and functional nature of facts, discussed earlier, it also suggests that all social and moral relations, along with the norms and values that mediate them, are existentially fixed, leaving no room for any selective appraisal of solutions in terms of what is objectively desirable.[5]

This exclusion of all evaluation from social inquiry, Dewey observes, is "effected only through the intermediary of a thoroughly fallacious notion...namely, that the moral blames and approvals . . . are evaluative and that they exhaust the field of evaluation" (490). In light of the strictly experimental and functional nature of all principles of inquiry, however, we must object that moral evaluations are not evaluative in any logical sense of judgment. They are not even judgments in the logical sense of judgment, for they rest upon some preconceptions of ends that should be or ought to be attained. This preconception excludes ends (consequences) from the field of inquiry and reduces inquiry at its very best to the truncated and distorted business of finding out means for realizing objectives already settled upon (490).

As in all inquiry, judgments in experimentally controlled inquiry institute "means-consequences (ends) in strict conjugate relation to each other," whereby the proposed (envisaged) ends themselves are nothing but procedural means for bringing about the resolution of existential conflicts. All procedural means, including the proposed ends and the existential, conceptual, and factual materials, must be "adjudged (evaluated)" strictly on the basis of the available evidence "of their power to exercise the function of resolution" (490; see also 117). In facts-based inquiry, as defined by social scientists, the interdependence of the procedural means for the resolution of social conflicts is ignored and a fundamental logical condition of all experimentally controlled inquiry violated. Without ends as directive procedural means, no potentially observable and recordable materials can be selected from "the big blooming buzzing confusion" of experience and weighed "as data or 'the facts of the case' " (491). And without the other procedural means, no directive ends could be projected in any responsible manner.

This and the other briefly reviewed sorry conditions encountered in social inquiry, I suggest, could be easily avoided by adopting the procedural and experimental principles that Dewey found operative in all successful and respectable inquiry. It would seem then that Dewey's test of the philosophical promise of his theory of inquiry is a success, and given his account, the situation in democratic social inquiry is bleak, but not hopeless, despite the ever growing tendency to interpret social troubles in moral terms.

Notes

1. For Dewey's comparison-contrast of the operational logic of modern science with the "the classical type of logic," see MW 4: 3 passim.

2. For a discussion of Kant's similar remarks about the influence of experimental science on his "treatise on method" (*The Critique of Pure Reason*), see Seigfried (1993, 2001). Here I go along with Dewey's neo-Kantian understanding of Kant's position.

3. It is tempting to take this demonstration as a good reason for dismissing *Logic* as uncritical scientism that is at odds with positions

defended in *Human Nature and Conduct* (MW 14) and *Art as Experience* (LW 10). However, have a look at the passage cited in the next section from LW 12: 481. It would be odd, indeed, if such conditions could be safely ignored, where the conflict of leading ideas in inquiry seems to be worst, and where we can least afford to trust uncontrolled intuition.

4. See also Dewey's remarks on the institution of problems: "Any problem of scientific inquiry that does not grow out of actual (or 'practical') social conditions is factitious; it is arbitrarily set by the inquirer instead of being objectively produced and controlled" (LW 12: 492).

5. T. H. Huxley, in his letter to Charles Kingsley, quoted by Stephen Jay Gould, (1984).

Works Cited

Boisvert, Raymond D. 1988. *Dewey's metaphysics.* New York: Fordham University Press.

Gould, S. J. 1984. Between you and your genes. *The New York Review of Books* 31 (August 16): 30–33.

Kant, I. [1781/A, 1787/B] 1965. *The critique of pure reason.* Translated by Norman Kemp Smith. New York: St Martin's Press.

Nietzsche, F. [1873] 1979. On truth and lies in a nonmoral sense." In *Philosophy and truth: Selections from Nietzsche's notebooks of the early 1870s,* ed. Daniel Breazeale, 79–91. Atlantic Highlands, NJ: Humanities Press.

Rorty, R. 1999. *Philosophy and social hope.* New York: Penguin Books.

Seigfried, H. 1993. Dewey's critique of Kant's Copernican Revolution revisited. *Kant-Studien* 83: 356–68.

———. 2001. Truth and Use. *Synthese* 128: 1–2: 1–13.

Sleeper, R. W. 1986. *The necessity of pragmatism: John Dewey's conception of philosophy.* New Haven, CT: Yale University Press.

Contributors

James Campbell is a distinguished university professor at the University of Toledo. He has been a Fulbright Lecturer at the University of Innsbruck (1990–91) and the University of Munich (2003–04). He is the author of many articles and several books, including *The Community Reconstructs: The Meaning of Pragmatic Social Thought* (1992), *Understanding John Dewey* (1995), and *A Thoughtful Profession: The Early Years of the American Philosophical Association* (2006). He is currently president of the Society for the Advancement of American Philosophy.

Jim Garrison is a professor of philosophy of education at Virginia Tech. He is the author of many book chapters, refereed papers, and books, including *Dewey and Eros* (Teachers College Record). Jim is a past winner of the Jim Merritt award for his scholarship in the philosophy of education and the John Dewey Society Outstanding Achievement Award. He is a past president of the Philosophy of Education Society and president of the John Dewey Society.

Judith Green is associate professor of philosophy and co-director of women's studies at Fordham University. She is the author of many book chapters and refereed papers, as well as two book-length works, *Deep Democracy: Community, Diversity, and Transformation* (1999) and *Pragmatism and Social Hope: Deepening Democracy in Social Contexts* (2008).

Charlene Haddock Seigfried is professor of Philosophy and American Studies and a member of the Women's Studies committee at Purdue University. Among her books are: *Pragmatism and Feminism* (1996) and *William James's Radical Reconstruction of Philosophy* (1990) and she edited *Feminist Interpretations of John Dewey* (2002). Recent work includes introductions to *Democracy and Social Ethics* and *The Long Road of Woman's Memory* in the Jane Addams series of the University of Illinois Press. Seigfried was awarded the 2005 John Dewey Society Outstanding Achievement Award. She is a past president of the Society for the Advancement of American Philosophy as well as of the William James Society.

Larry A. Hickman is Director of the Center for Dewey Studies and professor of philosophy at Southern Illinois University, Carbondale. He is the author of *Modern Theories of Higher Level Predicates* (1980), *John Dewey's Pragmatic Technology* (1990), and *Philosophical Tools for Technological Culture* (2001), as well as the editor of *Technology as a Human Affair* (1990), *Reading Dewey* (1998), *The Essential Dewey* (with Thomas Alexander, 1998), and the three-volume *The Correspondence of John Dewey*, (1999, 2001, 2005). Hickman has published dozens of essays on a wide variety of topics. He has served as president of the Society for the Advancement of American Philosophy and the John Dewey Society.

Stefan Neubert is an associated member (Oberstudienrat im Hochschuldienst) of the teaching staff of the Faculty of Humanities at the Universität zu Köln, director of the Office for International Relations, and member of the executive committee of the Dewey Center at the Universität zu Köln. His research focuses on Interactive Constructivism, Deweyan pragmatism, philosophy of education, and theories of culture and communication. He is the author of over twenty-five papers and a book on the philosophy of John Dewey and coeditor of four books in German, including one on Dewey and Interactive Constructivism, which has been translated into English (forthcoming, 2008).

Kersten Reich is a professor at the Universität zu Köln and the founder of Interactive Constructivism, a brand of constructivism that stands in close proximity to pragmatism (especially Deweyan pragmatism). He is the director of the Dewey Center at the Universität zu Köln, the author of many papers book and chapters, and the author or editor of sixteen books, including one on Dewey and Interactive Constructivism, which has been translated into English.

Hans Seigfried (1933–2006) was a professor of philosophy at Loyola University of Chicago and was the first director of the department's graduate program in continental philosophy. He served on the Committee on International Cooperation of the American Philosophical Association and on the Executive Committee of the Society for the Advancement of American Philosophy, and he was cofounder and director of the Midwest Pragmatist Study Group. The author of many book chapters and refereed papers, he also is the author of *Wahrheit und Metaphysik bei Suarez* (Bouvier Verlag). He presented many papers internationally, including in Poland, France, and Germany, among other nations.

Index